Homosexuality and Christian Faith

Homosexuality and Christian Faith

Questions of Conscience for the Churches

edited by
Walter Wink

Fortress Press
Minneapolis

HOMOSEXUALITY AND CHRISTIAN FAITH
Questions of Conscience for the Churches

Cover design: Craig Claeys
Interior design: Beth Wright

The authors, editor, and publisher gratefully acknowledge the assistance and permission of Pendle Hill Publications (for Elise Boulding's essay excerpted from *One Small Plot of Heaven*); Wm. B. Eerdman's Publ. Co. (for materials adapted from Lewis Smedes, *Sex for Christians*); *The Baptist Peacemaker* (for Ken Sehested's essay, there titled "St. Peter and the Jerusalem Protocol"); and Via Media Services (for Bp. Paul Egertson's essay).

Library of Congress Cataloging-in-Publication Data

Homosexuality and Christian faith : questions of conscience for the
    churches / edited by Walter Wink.
        p. cm.
        Includes bibliographical references.
        ISBN 0-8006-3186-2 (alk. paper)
        1. Homosexuality—Religious aspects—Christianity. I. Wink,
    Walter.
    BR115.H6H634 1999
    261.8'35766—dc21   99-22979
                                                                        CIP

Manufactured in the U.S.A.   AF 1-3186
    03   02   01   00   99   1   2   3   4   5   6   7   8   9   10

Contents

مجه

Preface

✍

Today the churches are undergoing fratricide over the issue of homosexuality, and the irony is that not just gays and lesbians, but the churches themselves, are likely to become the victims. The level of pure hatred, bitterness, closemindedness, and disrespect is staggering, going beyond any form of acrimony I have witnessed over any issue since the struggle against racial segregation.

This book aims to shine light into that darkness. Its authors have, in the past, led us through one difficult moral test after another: the civil rights movement, the Vietnam War, resistance to nuclear power and nuclear war, the struggle against apartheid, the exploitation of developing countries, the oppression of women, opposition to the religious right. Time after time they have been out in front and alone, sometimes assailed as traitors, pinkos, communists, lawbreakers, harebrained idealists. And time after time their wisdom has been belatedly confirmed by the churches.

I believe they are right on this issue as well, and that we should listen to these guides. They have proven to be prophets before. They could be wrong this time, but I think it unlikely that all of them are wrong. All I ask of the reader is a fair reading. The writers are a mix of evangelicals, conservatives, and liberals, with a number who reject all such labeling in regard to themselves. I believe that they represent the church at its best, struggling for clarity on this tortured issue, and that what they say will be confirmed by the church of the future.

Several of the contributors speak personally about children, classmates, colleagues, and friends who are gay (Shriver, Shields, Egertson). Conscious of the human cost of same-sex orientation in our society, we then turn to face head-on the task of interpreting Scripture around this contentious issue (Wink, Sehested). But the very ambiguity of Scripture and the suffering of gays and lesbians requires that we look to the human sciences and Christian ethics for additional light on the issue (Kelsey, Myers, Harris and Moran, Smedes). This examination leads us to reassess our Christian tradition (Rohr, Cobb) and challenge the churches to recover their prophetic vocation (Campolo, Coffin, Boulding). We conclude with the practical questions of ordaining gays and lesbians, blessing their unions, and granting them not only full human rights, but whole-hearted acceptance in our churches (Castuera, Siler).

Despite the amount of heat the debate over homosexuality has produced in the churches, the discussion has been woefully slack as far as rigorous theological thinking is concerned. The sheer passion of the discussion betrays emotionalism on both sides, and the necessary exegetical and theological grounding is ignored.

It is my hope, and that of all the contributors, that this volume will help bring serious reflection and a loving approach to this controversy. We stand, blessed, before this stupendous gift—the mystery of human sexuality—awed, confused, and rendered delicate toward ourselves and others as we seek to listen closely to the new things the Spirit is saying to the churches.

—*Walter Wink*

Introduction

More Light from the Spirit on Sexuality

James A. Forbes Jr.

∽

James Forbes has been, since 1989, the senior minister of the Riverside Church in New York City, the first African American to serve as senior minister at one of the largest multicultural congregations in the nation. An ordained minister in the American Baptist Churches and the Original United Holy Church of America, he has served several pastorates and taught homiletics at Union Theological Seminary, New York City. At Union he is the first Harry Emerson Fosdick Adjunct Professor of Preaching while serving on the core teaching staff at Auburn Theological Seminary. In 1986 he delivered the Lyman Beecher Lectures at Yale University, published as *The Holy Spirit and Preaching* (1989). *Newsweek* named him one of the twelve "most effective preachers" in the English-speaking world in 1996. *Ebony* magazine designated him as one of America's greatest black preachers in 1984 and 1993.

∽

> I still have many things to say to you, but you cannot bear them now. When the Spirit of truth comes, that Spirit will guide you into all the truth. For the Spirit will not speak independently but will speak whatever the Spirit hears and will declare to you the things that are to come. This Spirit will glorify me by taking what is mine and declaring it to you. All that God has is mine. For this reason I said that the Spirit will take what is mine and declare it to you.
>
> (John 16:12-15)

I want to say to you, each and every one, that it is no longer off-limits for sexual topics to be discussed in the church or from the pulpit. Everybody else is talking about it. Television shows, magazine racks, kids behind the wall. So why not in church?

As a norm of our gathering, we understand that sex is a gift of God. Sex was such that God spoke of it along with the rest of the creation, saying, "And it is good." Sex, both individual and intimate, private and yet, in ways, framed by social norms, is a part of the fabric of our shared existence. Sex. I'm saying it enough to get used to it. Sex. Physical. Mental. Spiritual. It is the expression of individual libido as well as individual conscience, and it is also a project that community attends to so that the well-being of all may be provided.

We need to talk about these things. It is not only appropriate to do so, but urgent, desperately urgent that we talk together about these things. For issues of sexuality are turning out to be a spiritual fault line threatening the stability and the unity of the church. These issues are fragmenting families, polarizing communities, and also affecting policies that claim to protect the liberties of all of the citizens of our democracy. These problems are with us, and, though we may have made some advances, now the general climate in society is filled with fear, anxiety, and confusion.

Religious traditions have spoken on these matters. Often the only thing you could hear was, Don't do it. Many, many times we have heard from our various traditions, rules, regulations, principles, and practices. People get really stirred up about these things. There is intensity in the debate. People actually leave churches on the basis of these conversations. They are not always so righteous themselves, nor is their behavior so exemplary. I think people get excited about their perspective on sexuality because it gives them the feeling that, their failures notwithstanding, if they take a hard stand on what they consider to be godly, maybe God will be more merciful to them.

You see, as a pastor for a long time, I have found only a few people who were as aware as I thought they might have been. Very few people could claim that they would get an A if God graded them on the process of their maturity into sexual, well, should I call it sexual rectitude? I guess that's okay. That there are very few people who would say,

Listen up, you-all, let me describe the trajectory of my life and the development of my sexual patterns in life and use me as Exhibit A. There are very few people who would volunteer that way. And do you know why? Because it's hard to develop fully as a sexual being and make all the right moves. In fact, part of the development is the decision you make one day to be in charge of what you're going to do with yourself and not have everybody else tell you, Oh, no, don't do this, don't do that.

It's a messy business, growing up. I think that's what we need to understand. Just like love is a messy business. It's hard to come forth without some portions that do not seem too attractive. So many people, if the truth were known, live their lives on two levels. The principles they fight about are often at odds with the complicated and often frustrated lives they live. This is why there is so much intensity.

So let me tell you what my agenda is. I would like us, first, to give some thought to the idea that the state should not interfere in relationships that are consummated, whether you call them bonding or marriage, whatever you call them, that the state has no right to deny people the opportunity to live out the concreteness of their commitments to one another. And second, that the church should support the idea that the benefits of marriage, whatever they are, are not to be denied persons of different orientations, whether they are gay or straight or lesbian, bisexual, transgender or what. There has to be equality in the way the church sets forth principles about how people should live and love and experience the sexual dimensions of life.

Usually, when there's a discussion of this nature, the people who already believe in what is called the Post-Sexual Revolution will be there. So most of these discussions are choir rehearsals. Rehearsing over and over and over what most of the people who are there already believe. That's a problem. That's a problem not only in this church, but all across the nation. The polarization is such that the conservatives on this side have their prayer meeting and their choir meeting. And the liberals on this side have their prayer meeting and their choir meeting, and the two sides never get together and talk about it. The result is the tearing apart of the fabric of the body of Christ.

Riverside Church has an inclusiveness doctrine that says we will not sit around and judge that someone who is different from us cannot be loved by God. We are positive in affirming all of our brothers and sisters here, whatever their sexual expression may be. We have made a great deal of progress, let me tell you. We had a wonderful scrimmage here for a while, and out of it came the doctrine. But the truth is that a good number of people suffered for it to be so. They felt that there was an integrity of faith that did not allow them to embrace this understanding. And we've had several very specific moments in which all is going well until you bring this topic up and then people lower their heads and say, Lord, oh Lord, how long? And the Lord says, I've been wondering how long it will take you to . . . no, not really. The truth of the matter is that we can decide that what we'll do is have a vote, and if the vote is 151 to 150, once again we have our policy.

But I'm standing here today to say that that is not good enough—a situation where politically we simply overpower people and say, This is it. We have a more difficult task before us, and that will not be completed until the members of this church can talk to each other about the perspective they have and why they do not see this and why they see that. We have done well and, yes, there are times when you have to vote and the vote sets the official policy. But in a pastoral spirit, it is never enough just to vote, and then thank God that the other people don't count. For as soon as we vote them to the margin, then they become the ones that in Christian sensitivity we pay closest attention to, because that is the essence of the Christian faith: namely, that we are the body and we pay special attention to those who have been marginalized. And who is on the margin changes from time to time in the light of political developments.

One of my burdens is being a person who came from an Evangelical and Pentecostal background, and so every time

I make a pronouncement here from this pulpit in this church that is called the bastion of liberalism, in this progressive whole-sexual-revolution-congregation, part of my mind is on the other folks who also are a part of the body of Christ.

How can we approach our work, not abandoning them, but bringing them along? How can we keep them from generating attitudes that result in the bashing of people, the killing of people, the denial of people's rights?

Some of you simply feel that same-gender marriage is wrong. You want us to be pleasing in God's sight, and this is the perspective you have always understood and this is where you stand, and you just feel you can't change. For those of us who like to think that we represent the good old days, I've got some advice for you. If you're talking about the good old days, please be specific about which of the good old days you're talking about. Are you talking about the good old days when slavery was condoned in the Bible and in society? Are you talking about the good old days when children were executed for disobeying their parents? Are you talking about the good old days when prophets of the Lord were instructed by the Lord to kill all the prophets of the other religious tradition? Are you talking about the good old days when women were required to be silent in the church? If so, go on back to the good old days!

But in the spirit of pastoral balance, does modern spirituality and post-sexual revolution mean that there are no norms anymore? Does the new day mean there are no restraints? No accountability to family, to covenant, to community? Is there no more superego, only the id? Does the new day mean no more discipline and I'll do what I want and it ain't nobody's business if I do just because I can? No, it's no longer good enough to say you're liberal or conservative. Those terms are confusing now. So, you've got to look up under the label, pardon the expression, and find out what you mean and what you believe to be Jesus' message to us.

My purpose is to start the conversation and not to end it. In our Scripture passage today, Jesus says to the disciples:

There are lots of things I want to say to you, but you are not able to understand what these things are. And the reason you don't understand is that answers to unasked questions don't really make a whole lot of sense. There are foundational principles that I have set forth, but I'm leaving now, and you're going to sit around and wonder, well, what did Jesus say about this and what did Jesus say about that? I have said nothing about some of those things in particular, so here's the arrangement I'm making—we are going to pray, and the heavenly Parent is going to send the Spirit. I have been with you, and you have been able to ask me all these questions, all the time, anything that came up, but now you will not have me there. But what will happen is this: I will send my Spirit, and my Spirit will come into your heart, and the Spirit will repeat everything that I have said and then elucidate it in the light of the developments in your time, so that in a contemporary setting you will know what it means to be a Christian and how you might apply Christian values to the difficult problems that we face under the new circumstances.

So I'm saying to you that the task of the church is to understand that Jesus didn't answer it all, and many of the things that had been said in the good old days, Jesus updated even in his time. You're not a violator of the gospel. Your Lord was the translator and transformer and reviser so that we could be revised to the heart of God's original intention. Every culture just does the best it can. But no culture can piggyback completely on the wisdom of a past culture. I would love to ask St. Augustine what he thought. I know he gave his best insights. But this is not St. Augustine's time, this is your time and my time, and Jesus expects us to open our hearts to the Spirit and raise some difficult questions before the Spirit.

We need more light from the Spirit on sexuality. Some things are different now. I can't do it by myself. I need the conservatives and the liberals, the old-timers and the newcomers. I need all of us to present these issues to the Spirit. Maybe some of you think you know the answers already, but the consensus is not there until your answers are clear enough that you can share it with others and bring us along in dialogue. We need to ask Jesus—no, don't ask Jesus. Ask the Spirit now: Holy Ghost, talk to us. Some things are different now from the other days. Jesus, when you were preaching in the old days, people assumed the sexuality thing was basically that God made everybody heterosexual in orientation. Now, Jesus, the scientists and other people are telling us that we were deceived in that. That just as the bodies in the heavens are different and the constellations are different, and just as in nature there are differences that we never noticed, that human beings are not all the same. That if you lined all of us up around the room, that we may be as different as you can imagine in our tastes, in our desires, in our approach, in what we would do with ourselves, in what would be a fulfilling relationship for us. Line us all up: even all of the straights are not the same. And all of the gay and lesbian, bisexual and transgendered folks don't have the same perspective. We are so different, and we ask the Holy Ghost: Holy Ghost, will you help us to walk around this circle and tell us, Holy Ghost, which ones of these you want us to put outside of the circle because they are an abomination in the sight of God? Holy Ghost, help us to see who ought to be excluded and who ought to be included.

I know it would be a shock to a person who had no sexual desires, who never had any sexual experience, who never even cared about the development of a strong friendship: "Well, I know I'm going to be in the circle because I never wanted anything, never did anything, and I know God loves me"—and the Holy Spirit says, Now this one we need to send back to the factory, because something is really wrong here! And so we have to ask the Holy Spirit: Holy Spirit, we understand that there is a genetic contribution to the nature of one's sexual and social desires. Did God do that, or is this just an aberration? Holy Spirit, we want to be careful what we say, because so much has been said. Is heterosexuality the preferred way for all? Is it that in nature a percentage will be homosexual, and did you make them for a reason? It would be interesting for the Holy Spirit to say: Well, at first the plan was to make everybody heterosexual, and then God thought that to counteract pride, people were going to have to learn how to make space for people who are different. So at the end the Lord says, "I'm going to put a few who are different in many different ways so that people will understand that God's love is not just for them."

Holy Spirit, help us, there are so many problems we're running into. The old folks can no longer bear children, and the Holy Spirit says: Wait a minute, don't forget the story of Abraham and Sarah. They were very old in years, but, Holy Spirit, in the nursing home where two people fall in love and where their benefits are going to be adversely affected if they get married, must they get married in order to look at each other and say, like the Song of Solomon, "Your breasts are clusters of dates . . . your breath as sweet as the fragrance of quince" (7:7-8)? Should they get married or not? And if they don't get married, tisk, tisk, tisk.

Also, Holy Spirit, I have promised to talk to the singles in this church. I have promised to preach a sermon, but you haven't given it to me yet, and so I can't go ahead. What am I to say? Holy Spirit, the good old days were heavy on premarital chastity. It was heavy on prohibiting even self-pleasuring. In the good old days, any kind of sex that was not likely to be procreative was denied a place in the family. In the old days, marital fidelity was the bottom line. Holy Spirit, what shall I say?

Holy Spirit, speak to us! How can we get around the double standard? We want the women to be virgins, but the men should have experience. Well, how can we come to justice on these matters?

Holy Spirit, I understand there was a tradition that when somebody got ready to marry that the priest came into the room the day they were to be married, and sex was consummated, and the priest waited and would not marry them unless there was on the sheet evidence that the woman was a virgin. We haven't figured out a way to tell whether the men are virgins, not yet.

Have I said enough to get the conversation started? We can discuss these matters, but we will discuss them in a context where we are free to express our opinions, because I am now convinced that a solid list of the principles by which we can have sound sexual understanding within the Christian faith will draw wisdom from both dimensions, and I look forward to being in a congregation where people are free to express themselves without political correctness disenfranchising them. And I look forward to justice moving among us so that those who are new to the margins will develop the power to be heard. We need to pay attention to those who now are the new occupants of the seats on the margin.

So would you allow me three principles just to start the conversation? One: Jesus says, A new commandment I give you, that you love one another. So whatever our sexual list will involve, can we learn to love each other from the heart? Second, there must be truth about it. Don't be trying to do something that's not who you are. I think the message is that, given the various differences, one of the hardest things we have to come to is, Who am I really? And remember the word of Jesus: You shall know the truth and the truth shall set you free. Don't come trying to be something that you think the culture wants you to be if it's not true. Take your truth to God and ask, God, help me work out how I deal with this truth and then please, please put justice in it. That's my third point. Please have a just principle that applies to those who are gay and those who are straight, equally, because all of us are members of the family of God. Let's build on the list, and one day we're going to have a wonderful time celebrating the list that has been compiled by conservatives and liberals, old-timers and newcomers, and it will be the standard by which all of us who are in the body of Christ can be one in the family with all our differences. God bless you.

Part One

Personal Encounters

I

A Belated Justice:
Reflections on an Unpaid Debt

Donald W. Shriver Jr.

⌐

Donald Shriver is president of the faculty and William E. Dodge Professor of Practical Christianity, emeritus, of Union Theological Seminary,
New York City. From 1972 to 1975 he served as Professor of Ethics and
Society at the Candler School of Theology at Emory University. He was
elected the thirteenth president of Union in 1975, holding that position
until 1991, when he returned to teaching. He has engaged in extensive
interdisciplinary dialogue, teaching, and writing, dealing with such
issues as Jewish and Christian dialogue, business and leadership ethics,
urban ministry, and religion and the media. He holds six honorary doctoral degrees, is a past president of the Society for Christian Ethics, and
is a member of the Council on Foreign Relations. His most recent books
are *The Business Corporation and Productive Justice* (1997) with David A.
Krueger and Laura L. Nash, *An Ethic for Enemies: Forgiveness in Politics*
(1995), and *Beyond Success: Corporations and Their Critics in the Nineties*
(1991) with James Kuhn. He and his wife, Peggy, have three children and
three grandchildren.

⌐

AIDS is not a "homosexual disease," but the trajectory of
its history in the past fifteen years has raised to view a
new version of an old moral issue: what are we to believe
about the varieties of being human, in light of societies' universal propensity for *classifying* their members?

There is apparently no escape from seeing other human
beings, initially at least, through classification lenses. Is
the other a man or a woman? Poor or rich? Native or foreign? White or black? Christian or Jew? And so on ad
infinitum, as we seek to satisfy our yen to get other folk

13

fixed into categories that are useful for instructing us in how to relate to them.

Different cultures have different conventional lenses, of course. For long it has been evident to me that in urban, corporate culture the first question at a cocktail party is usually, "What do you do?" In my native South the first question was more likely to be, "Where are you from?" But when Southerners want to really get acquainted with each other, they ask, "Who are your people?"

There is human wisdom and danger to humanity in that latter question. On its face, it is a powerful classifier, suggesting the rule, "You shall know them by their relations," in this case their families of origin. There is something wise in the rule, wiser than the typical American individualist wants to admit. But there is something ethically dangerous, too; for the question tempts us to put our feet on that long sad journey toward dividing the whole of humanity into "us" and "them."

Does it make any sense even to talk about "the whole of humanity"? It has to make sense, if one means to take a slant on one's species compatible with the Bible. In both its Hebrew and Christian sections, a trek from provincial to comprehensive slants on "the human" gets clearly traced. Who can read the books of Second Isaiah, Ruth, and Jonah without feeling a tide of true humanism breaking through the walls of provincialism in the life of Israel? Who can understand Jesus' dealings with the social outcast or the turn toward gentile inclusiveness in the early church without discerning the Holy Spirit's conquest of the myriad "dividing walls of hostility" that our history has reared up in the architecture of our societies?

Martin Buber translated the second half of the Great Commandment, "You shall love your neighbor as a person like yourself," proposing thereby a great and painful transition from classification addiction to discernment of the humanity in "all sorts and conditions" of our neighbors and proposing, too, an inclusivist answer to the question, "Who are your people?" Matt. 12:46-50 has Jesus' radical answer to that one! "Whoever does the will of my Father in heaven is my brother and sister and mother."

But acting on that idea involves an experiential journey, not just the adoption of an idea. All of us begin as provincials; we have to be shaken out of our provincialism by experiences of the stranger who, only over time and in interchange, becomes a neighbor who is indeed a person like oneself. Matt. 15:21-28 seems to say that about Jesus, who had to learn to treat a Syro-Phoenecian woman as a neighbor.

Most of us have to concede that our experience of actually relating to strangers has dug at the subsoils of our own walls of hostility as frequently as have our abstract ideas. For native white Southerners like myself, an experience of co-humanity with black Southerners was our first training in meeting the larger challenge of world pluralism. In that pluralism reside a group of neighbors who publicly claim their right to be considered fully human: gays and lesbians.

The hearing of that rightful claim has been a slow process in my life as a heterosexual, and doubtless there is much that I still need to hear. Worth recounting is one incident in my biography that, in an early year, alerted me to the deep evil of a society that morally condemns one of its sexual "classes." Since that early year, and especially in the past twenty years, I have been colleague, friend, or acquaintance with no small number of gay neighbors, but my personal commitment to learning with them "how to be human now" (W. H. Auden) took shape first in connection with a friend whose struggle with his own sexual identity ended in tragedy. It was in that tragedy that I first learned that the social affirmation of gay and lesbian people is a life-and-death issue.

As an army draftee in 1946 I became vaguely aware that there was such a thing as homosexuality. But in those days barracks talk hid the subject under veils of crude slurs; who could learn anything real about it in that atmosphere? Then one day at Fort Monmouth, New Jersey, I met M. Frank Reid Jr. from Laurens, South Carolina. Not only did we strike up vigorous theological conversations, but when, soon after, he was transferred to cryptographic school in San Francisco—a specialty reserved for soldiers of high I.Q.—we began a flourishing six-year correspondence.

In that correspondence, in the books we exchanged, and in our occasional visits in each other's home cities, we explored all the deep subjects that Southern Presbyterians and Southern Baptists, headed for seminary, are likely to explore. Especially after he entered Harvard, his letters and gifts introduced me to poets, philosophers, and theologians about whom I had hardly heard: W. H. Auden, Migel de Unamuno, Martin Buber, Paul Tillich, and Reinhold Niebuhr. Niebuhr's annual preaching at the Harvard Memorial Chapel grew into an academic friendship that brought Frank in 1951 to Union Seminary in New York, just as I was entering the school of the same name in Virginia.

Looking back at it, I realize that there were a few "blips" on the wide screen of our friendship that might have alerted me to a trouble that Frank Reid kept hidden from almost all of his friends—and he had many. One Christmas I gave him a copy of Harry Emerson Fosdick's book, *On Being a Real Person*. He received the gift with overtones of jocularity, but with the suggestion that maybe I did not consider him a real person. There was a side of him, I would later learn, that he was sharing with only one other male friend and with his psychiatrist.

I shall always wonder if, in the months just before my marriage, my obvious joy in that anticipation was one of many influences that added up to his desperate decision to end his life in the spring of 1953. His suicide was so traumatic for Union students that the collective wisdom of Reinhold Niebuhr, Paul Tillich, Bill Webber, Robert Handy, and Pitney Van Dusen was hardly sufficient to deal with the mixed surplus and scarcity of meaning that students were tempted to attribute to it.

In fact, the chief meaning of his death did not become clear to a wide circle of his friends until years later. In my case, only in 1961, in a conversation with Reinhold and

Ursula Niebuhr during his year as a visiting professor at Harvard, was I informed of the root of Frank's problem: he was gay, and he could discover no social space, in a seminary or anywhere else in the context of 1953 America, in which he could be the real person he was and wanted to be.

Twenty-two years later, soon after I had accepted the unlikely invitation to become thirteenth president of Union, one member of the seminary board, T. Guthrie Speers Jr., and I enjoyed the immediate bond of having been friends of Frank Reid. "He would have been a good president of Union," I commented. "Yes," said Guthrie, "and if he had lived . . . who knows?" Not until the fall of 1990 did I ever speak a public word about the esteem and sorrow in my friendship with the one Union student whom I knew well in 1953.

By 1975, the gay rights movement was well under way, and Union was becoming one of the places where the humanity of gays and lesbians was coming out of the social closet. My understanding of homosexuality was not profound; it still isn't. But from the beginning of my long tenure as Union president, I determined that part of my vocation there was to cultivate its ethos as a place where all sorts and conditions of humans were welcome, whether we yet understood each other or not. If we did not welcome each other, how could we even begin to understand? The autobiographical impetus behind that commitment was what I *could* understand about Frank Reid's suicide: it was a tragic waste of a life full of brilliance, compassion, and promise for the service of the church and the world. Frank was one reason that I finally came to see that how society treats *any* of its alleged "deviants" is a life-and-death matter.

Who are the deviants? Our early education convinces us that it is possible and necessary to know. Perhaps our later education convinces us that it is not so possible, necessary, or desirable as once we were taught to believe. A certain reserve, a certain agnosticism about how any human neighbor ought to be classified, may comport best with what we already know about ourselves—that we have much yet to know. If, with Paul, we are willing to admit that empirically, in many dimensions of our experience, "we do not understand our own actions," who are we to pretend we know others well enough to fit them securely into some pigeonhole role? And if, with Jesus, we accept the vocation of affirming the humanity of society's rejects, we are likely to find ourselves, like Jesus, the enemy of every wall of hostility between "them" and "us."

In hailing the entry of the United Presbyterian Church into the struggle for civil rights, Eugene Carson Blake spoke the memorable words, "We come late; late, we come." The gay rights movement came too late for Frank Reid, and I have often reflected that had it come earlier, it might have saved his life. Who knows how many lives it has now saved from that form of premature death that is social contempt? Over the past forty years I have at last come to know many gay persons, counted many of them friends, and learned from them new urgency for combat on the frontiers of my own prejudices. But the door that opened me to these friendships and that fired me for this combat was M. Frank Reid Jr. Belatedly, with gratitude, I write these paragraphs in his honor.

2

Thoughts from the Weekend of the Quilt

Carole Shields

↙⌐

Carole Shields is president of People For the American Way, a 300,000-member organization that supports freedom of conscience and expression, civic participation, equality, justice, tolerance, and diversity. While vice president of Hospice Care, Inc., she developed the nation's largest hospice program for persons living with AIDS. The reflections that follow focus on the "Weekend of the Quilt," October 11–12, 1996 in Washington, D.C., which involved a display of the Names Project Quilt and celebrated the lives of victims of AIDS. It is dedicated to Art Kropp, her friend and predecessor at "People For," who died of AIDS in June 1993.

↙⌐

I started, of course, searching for the oak tree under whose branches lay the fabric stars that we stitched in our conference room for our own beloved Art. I ran into a former employee there, weeping; she had brought her mother, and I had a precious moment to tell the mother how wonderful I think her daughter is. And thus my day began, a day of grief and joy and feeling embraced by a community of suffering and caring. And everywhere around me, sewn in color and sunlight, were the darkest of our nights.

From the pieces of the quilt:
"If you listen you may hear him in the silence of the night,
Telling us that we may cry now. . . .
We'll find peace in his memories."
Written on a pair of jeans stitched to the quilt:
"I never could find your parents, so if anyone sees this who knows them, please tell them. . . ."

All day at the microphone, loving voices read names from a list and then added with even more feeling the names of those they had themselves loved and lost.

And at a distance a group of those filled with hate marched and chanted, "We are the holy union."

As evening approached, a stream of couples and families and single mourners poured toward the Capitol. And then came the candles, thousands and thousands melding together to march in memory. Flickers and tears; every age and color and language, marching as one, grieving as one, hoping as one, remembering together, and sharing the agonies of our pasts and the fear of how many times we might have to do this again.

As I looked out over the seemingly endless quilt, I thought of the many people I've known whose names are there. I decided my heart couldn't stand visiting all of their panels, and so I decided to look for Eddie and let his memory represent so many others of my friends and patients. When I found his panel, it wasn't the one I remembered, the one he insisted must include a rainbow. At first I was troubled by what happened to the panel I remembered, and I was puzzled by who might have done this one. And then I realized how many more people had been affected by his death than just those three of us who placed our hands on his bare chest for his last breaths. Maybe his parents had actually come through.

"Remember their names." Most of us who walked among the names clearly were there because we *do* remember and will always. But as panel after panel reached up to us as we tried to pass, we came to realize how many there are for whom we must be the surrogate rememberers, because their own mourners are lying there in the grass as well—sometimes side by side, but more often scattered and no longer connected in this world to their loved ones. And so as we walked, we adopted them and smiled to know them and ached from losing them, and we moved on to understand just how many of our own, and how much of ourselves, are remembered here.

The Names Project dinner on Friday night was an explosion of beauty. The roses, the strong faces, the tuxedos and glitter, the bonds of friendship, reminders everywhere of the generosity of the term "family," the candles and songs and celebrations of those who dedicate the texture of their days to making sure we remember. There was constant celebration of those who had lived long enough for this weekend, and there was the vaguely hollow look in the otherwise joyful eyes of those who don't know when their bodies will begin to betray them. There was celebration of life everywhere, laden with the richness that emerges only when we realize how fragile we are. And then there was the touching—everyone, everywhere, all around, and without fear. And all of us wearing little pins that said simply, "Remember."

There are two families in particular I will remember from this weekend. They are of both the traditional biological and the sociological construct. On Saturday at the quilt, there was a mother and father and two young sons, each of the boys under ten years old. As the father stood stunned in silence and the mother struggled to keep her flowing tears controlled, she reminded her boys about the days when the four of them worked together on this panel for their big brother. and she struggled to help them recall the precious things about this other son.

There was another family who stood across the street from the site of the dinner on Friday night. With bullhorn and ugly signs and quotations twisted from the Bible, they stood together to hurl religious obscenities—ultimate blasphemies—at those who arrived in love.

The panels of the quilt are decorated with references to things our lost ones enjoyed: sailboats and motorcycles, balloons and rainbows, music and dancing shoes, blue jeans and pink T-shirts. Symbols of the military and law enforcement and academia and medicine—certificates of honorable discharge, medals and stripes, caps and jackets, an appointment certificate to the D.C. Court of Appeals, and the cover page of a Ph.D. dissertation in botany. Symbols of childhood—teddy bears and tiny little dresses of little girls gone.

And everywhere, everywhere, symbols of faith. A cantor's robe; crosses of every sort in every color and fabric; messages from every possible religious tradition. One said, "Lieutenant Colonel, Reverend, Pastor, Man of God, Friend." Another: "We walk in love as Christ has loved us; Ephesians 5." The recurrent references to people who lived their lives in service to others told a caregiving community's story. Everywhere there were panels for nurses and doctors and chaplains and nursing assistants who stood watch for so many others and who were then remembered for their care.

At the Lincoln Memorial on Saturday night, a parade of men and women and children came to the microphone to say a few words that always included, "I am the face of AIDS." Finally, together, tens of thousands of candles were extinguished in an instant and replaced by a single giant torch flaming toward the sky. Quietly, reluctantly, we drifted away. We left knowing so much more than we had before just by being together in all our diversity and number and shared emotion. And our grief was both deepened and lessened by sharing it with so many others who understand.

On Sunday, I found myself back again, sitting under Art's tree. The weather was perfect, the tree providing shade and protection from the glare and heat; the branches cast shadows that gently brushed his name. I thought I might just sit there all day; I couldn't imagine a better place to be than keeping vigil there. As always, I kept thinking I'll somewhere find the instruction manual that surely he must have left for me.

One of the 12,000 volunteers who worked that day leaned down to offer me tissues. After a while, I realized that the glare was in my eyes, time had passed, the earth had moved, and the shade we shared was gone.

We *will* remember. And we will work to reflect the honor of his life.

3

One Family's Story

Bishop Paul Wennes Egertson

لا>

Paul Egertson attended Pepperdine College and Luther Seminary and earned a Ph.D. in theology and culture at the Claremont School of Theology in California. He served as director of the Center for Theological Study in Thousand Oaks, California, from 1979 to 1992. While an assistant professor of religion at California Lutheran University, he shared time as pastor of St. Matthew's Lutheran Church in North Hollywood. From 1995 to the present he has been bishop of the ELCA, Southern California West Synod. He and his wife, Shirley, have been married for more than forty years. They have six sons and five grandchildren. His sermons have been published in *Open Hands* (1996), *Augsburg Sermons: Series A Gospels* (1983), and *Augsburg Sermons: Minor Festivals* (1977). He has received several awards of distinction, including one for excellence in teaching in the adult degree evening program at California Lutheran University, and one as World's Greatest Dad on Father's Day 1986, from six boys with short memories.

لا>

What do you say after someone you love says, "I'm gay"? That's the question our family faced in 1978 when the oldest of our six sons told his mother and me that he is gay. That's the question Christian church families now face as more and more of our lesbian and gay members muster the courage to publicly share what they have privately known to be true for years.

My wife, Shirley, and I share our family story here, not because it is unique, but because it is a typical account of one way parents respond to the news that a child they love and admire is gay. We offer it with the prayer that it may help other families and our church family as we seek to understand a reality that will not go away. Looking back now, we can see seven periods of creative development in the transformation we have experienced.

DAY 1: DENY IT
Upon hearing the news our son brought us, our first reaction was to deny it. Admittedly, we knew very little about homosexuality at that time. After all, what was there to know? God created people male and female for the purpose of reproducing the human race and provided marriage as the proper setting for it. Sexual activity between people of the same sex was obviously a distortion of nature prohibited by both Scripture and common sense. What more does one need to know than that?

While we knew very little about homosexuality, we knew a great deal about our son. He didn't fit the image we had of a homosexual at all. He had been a delightful child to raise: bright as a whip and multitalented, self-directed and self-disciplined, honest and ethical to a fault, helpful and caring toward others. He graduated from high school with honors and from California Lutheran University with highest honors. Beyond that, he was a devoutly Christian young man, planning to enter the ordained ministry of the Lutheran Church like his grandfather and father before him, not from any pressure to maintain a family tradition, but out of a deep inner sense of call. In other words, he was as ideal a child as Christian parents could hope for in a world where nobody is perfect. We thought, "If he thinks he is gay, he must just be going through a phase of some kind, and when the right girl comes along he will resolve it. In the meantime, let's all keep our heads and not panic!"

The fact that he had not sexual relations with another man was a comfort to us and lent support to our denial of the conclusion to which he had come. But with the passing of time it became as clear to us as it was to him that this denial could not be maintained.

DAY 2: EXPLAIN IT

When we could no longer deny it, we sought to *explain it.*
How had such a fine young man become gay? What caused
it? Our state of ignorance was such that only two options
seemed possible. Either he had chosen a style of life in con-
tradiction to nature and the will of God, or his mother and
I, in our parenting, had unknowingly contributed to a dis-
torted development of his sexuality. Since we could not
convince ourselves that this highly ethical boy had sud-
denly chosen a deviant way of being, the fault must have
been our inadequacy as parents. Either his mother had
emasculated him by smother love, or I had been a weak
and/or too much absent father. We explored that explana-
tion for a while but, self-serving as the conclusion was, we
could not realistically see where that had been true in our
case. So we went in search of other explanations, and it was
here that our education began.

We learned there are several theories on the causes of
homosexuality, that they stand in conflict with each other,
that none of them can be sufficiently established to produce
a consensus, and that the only certain truth at this point in
time is that *nobody really knows.* The fact is that across time,
nations, classes, races, and cultures, a consistent percentage
of people in all populations are homosexual and the fault
cannot be laid at anyone's feet. We learned that nobody
knows what causes heterosexuality, either.

DAY 3: FIX IT

When we could neither deny it nor explain it, we sought to
fix it. There were two options open: divine intervention and
psychological therapy. As a devout Christian who knew
from early childhood that something was very different
about him and who suspected from adolescence that this
difference was something unacceptable to God, our son
had devoted himself to prayer and trust in the grace and
power of God. Preachers said God loved all people uncon-
ditionally and could change persons who came with a broken and contrite heart. So for years, night after night in the

privacy of his closet, he took his broken and contrite heart to the throne of grace, praying for God to change him. But God did not change him. Did that mean he was so defective that even a gracious God did not love him? What else is a teenage mind to conclude?

Since divine intervention did not occur, we pursued psychological therapy, only to discover that most psychiatrists and psychologists had long since come to the conclusion that homosexuality is not an illness and that no known system of treatment can change it. Homosexual *behavior* can be changed by conditioning people to be celibate or even to function heterosexually. *But the inner affectional orientation of constitutional homosexuals does not change.* And that was the issue for us, because sexual activity was not the problem. In short, there was no known way to fix it. The best that therapy can do is help gay and lesbian persons accept the reality of their being before the socially imposed shame and the personal pain drive them to despair, drink, drugs, or death by suicide, all of which it does daily to numerous persons in our world.

Day 4: Mourn it

When you can't deny it, explain it, or fix it, the only thing left is to *mourn it*. Parents have two choices at this point, both of which involve some form of death. On the one hand, you can choose the death of rejection and separation from your child. You can say, *If that's the way you are, you are no son of mine!* You can cut off relations as though the child never lived or as though the child has died. That's an option many parents have taken and an option congregations have regularly chosen in response to their lesbian and gay members. But quite frankly, that was never even an option for us, because we could not believe this son we knew so well was in any sense a perverted person.

The other choice is to suffer the death of your own misunderstandings, ignorance, and attitudes. Then you mourn the loss of a nice and tidy view of the world in which everything fits neatly into boxes of black or white, right or wrong, true or false. And, as a Christian, you mourn the loss of security provided by a few biblical passages that can tell you which is which so you don't have to take any responsibility for making a judgment.

Along with those losses goes the death of your hopes and dreams of ordinary happiness for your child, particularly as that comes through the joys of marriage, children, and a life approved by family, friends, church, and society. In our son's case, there is also the probable death of any hope for ordination into the ministry to which he has always felt called by God, unless he is willing to sacrifice for it all experiences of love expressed through human affection and physical intimacy.

During the process of this mourning, Shirley and I came to realize how close we were to shifting the focus from our son's struggle to our own. The final form of death for parents is to recognize that their pain is secondary to their child's suffering and to take up their role as supporters of the life they brought into the world, the life their child has to live out in the world. When that happened for us, the question became, *How is he handling this in terms of his own life, faith, health, and happiness?* It is his problem, not ours. He doesn't need us to increase his struggle by making the problem our own and then asking him to resolve it for us.

Day 5: Accept it
When our son came to the place where he could affirm the reality of his sexual orientation as given, we were able to open our minds and accept it. It was at this point we remembered the Serenity Prayer:

> Lord give us the serenity to accept what cannot be changed;
> the courage to change what can be changed;
> and the wisdom to know the difference.

For us that has come to mean the acceptance of something in the being of our son that neither we nor he would have chosen, something neither he nor we can change. More than that, it has come to mean seeking change in those things that can be changed, namely the attitudes toward

and understandings of homosexuality that remain dominant in both church and society. For we have come to realize *the biggest problem in being gay is not the gayness, but the
reaction of heterosexuals to it.* We want to join our voices with
those of others who seek the way of healing and wholeness
at this point of pain in our world.

As parents, we want to publicly express our thankful-
ness to the pastors and members of St. Francis Lutheran
Church in San Francisco, where our son experienced again
the gospel of reconciliation in both word and action
through which the Holy Spirit has kept him *united with
Jesus Christ in the one true faith.* Our prayer is that every
Christian parent of gay or lesbian children can someday be
assured their children will find that same gospel acceptance
in any congregation they may enter.

Day 6: Celebrate it

At this point in our transformation we have experienced a
sixth stage of development: *celebrate it!* Is that even possible? It all depends on what you think homosexuality is. To
what may it be rightly compared? Your answer to that
question will finally determine the place you stand. At least
four options are offered for your consideration.

First, you might say homosexuality is a conscious and
defiant rebellion against the laws of God and nature. In that
case, it is a problem of immoral behavior, like prostitution. If
that is true, our only proper response is trial and punishment,
on the one hand, and the announcement of God's judgment,
the offer of grace, and a call for repentance, on the other. But
is homosexuality rightly compared to prostitution?

A second option is to say that homosexuality is an illness
in which certain behaviors bring the bondage of addiction
that can be broken only by total abstinence. In that case, it
is like alcoholism, where the problem is not the internal
condition but the external behavior of drinking. If that's
true, then celibacy is clearly a sufficient solution to the
homosexual problem. But is homosexuality rightly compared to alcoholism?

A third option is to say that homosexuality is a tragedy in nature, something neither intended by God nor in harmony with God's will, but something that happens regularly in our world nonetheless. In that case, it is one of the tragic effects of the Fall, like infertility. That too is an unchangeable condition for which the victim is not responsible, but a condition we would never call good. If that's true, then shouldn't we treat homosexuals with the same compassion we grant to others who innocently suffer as victims of a fallen world? Shouldn't we make special rules for them so their lives can be as full as possible within the limits of their handicap?

When people have a physical disability and cannot walk, we don't conclude that God doesn't want them to move. Rather, we provide wheelchairs as substitute legs and set aside special parking spaces that are legal for them but illegal for others. When people are infertile, we don't conclude God doesn't want them to be parents. Rather, we arrange adoptions. Then shouldn't we provide gay and lesbian persons with a parallel structure to marriage that can allow them to experience the personal fulfillment produced by love expressed in approved relationships? But is homosexuality rightly compared to infertility?

The final option is to say that homosexuality is a variety in nature, one of those delightful differences that regularly appear in counterpoint to the ordinary norm. In that case, it is like left-handedness, a minority condition in a world where most people are right-handed and a few are ambidextrous, but a natural variation having its own contribution to make to the wholeness of the world.

There was a time when society considered left-handedness so deviant it had to be punished and changed. But in trying to force such change we discovered the same thing we're finding with gays and lesbians today: attempts to change them don't succeed but only cause more serious problems. Once that became clear in regard to left-handedness, we were freed to discover some positive benefits southpaws offer the world. Professional baseball teams, for example, value them highly. You can't win a championship without some lefties. Is homosexuality rightly compared to *left-handedness*? If so, we can *celebrate it* as a gift of God.

Since there are no experts who can answer these questions beyond the shadow of doubt, all we can do is digest the best information available from the testimony of gay and lesbian people, the ongoing results of scientific research, and the insights of serious biblical scholarship, praying that the Holy Spirit will lead us into truth. In the meantime, we all walk by faith and run with risk. Each of us will place our own bet and take responsibility for the outcome. As for me and my house, we're putting our money on the *celebration* line. We would rather err on the side of helping hurting people than on the side of hurting helpless people. *Lord, have mercy upon us!*

DAY 7: REST

Part Two

~

Biblical Witness

4

Homosexuality and the Bible

Walter Wink

↵⊃

Walter Wink is Professor of Biblical Interpretation at Auburn Theological Seminary. He has also taught at Union Theological Seminary, Hartford Seminary, and Columbia and Drew Universities. In 1989–90 he was a Peace Fellow at the United States Institute of Peace in Washington, D.C. His published works include a trilogy on the Powers: *Naming the Powers* (1984), *Unmasking the Powers* (1986), and *Engaging the Powers* (1992). *Engaging the Powers* received three Religious Book of the Year awards in 1993. A condensed version of the Powers trilogy was published in 1998 as *The Powers That Be*. He is also the author of almost 200 articles. He has led workshops all over North America, as well as in South Africa, Northern Ireland, East Germany, South Korea, New Zealand, and South and Central America. He is a United Methodist minister, works for a Presbyterian seminary, and attends Quaker meeting.

↵⊃

Sexual issues are tearing our churches apart today as never before. The issue of homosexuality threatens to fracture whole denominations, as the issue of slavery did a hundred and fifty years ago. We naturally turn to the Bible for guidance and find ourselves mired in interpretative quicksand. Is the Bible able to speak to our confusion on this issue?

The debate over homosexuality is a remarkable opportunity, because it raises in an especially acute way how we interpret the Bible, not in this case only, but in numerous others as well. The real issue here, then, is not simply homosexuality, but how Scripture informs our lives today.

Some passages that have been advanced as pertinent to the issue of homosexuality are, in fact, irrelevant. One is the attempted gang rape in Sodom (Gen. 19:1-29). That was a case of ostensibly heterosexual males intent on humiliating strangers by treating them "like women," thus demasculinizing them. (This is also the case in a similar account in Judges 19–21.) Their brutal behavior has nothing to do with the problem of whether genuine love expressed between consenting adults of the same sex is legitimate or not. Likewise Deut. 23:17-18 must be pruned from the list, since it most likely refers to male and female *prostitutes* involved in Canaanite fertility rites that have infiltrated Israelite worship; whether these males are "gay" or "straight," a mature same-sex love relationship is not under discussion.

Several other texts are ambiguous. It is not clear whether 1 Cor. 6:9 and 1 Tim. 1:10 refer to the "passive" and "active" partners in homosexual relationships, or to homosexual and heterosexual male prostitutes. In short, it is unclear whether the issue is homosexuality alone, or promiscuity and "sex for hire."

Unequivocal Condemnations

Putting these texts to the side, we are left with three references, all of which unequivocally condemn homosexual behavior. Lev. 18:22 states the principle: "You [masculine] shall not lie with a male as with a woman; it is an abomination" (NRSV). The second (Lev. 20:13) adds the penalty: "If a man lies with a male as with a woman, both of them have committed an abomination; they shall be put to death; their blood is upon them."

Such an act was regarded as an "abomination" for several reasons. The Hebrew prescientific understanding was that male semen contained the whole of nascent life. With no knowledge of eggs and ovulation, it was assumed that the woman provided only the incubating space. Hence the spilling of semen for any nonprocreative purpose—in coitus interruptus (Gen. 38:1-11), male homosexual acts, or male masturbation—was considered tantamount to murder. Female homosexual acts were consequently not so seriously regarded and are not mentioned at all in the Old

Testament (but compare Rom. 1:26). (For rabbinic censure of masturbation, see *b. Niddah* 13a and *b. Sanhedrin* 54b.) But Israelites also affirmed sexual intercourse for pleasure and companionship and permitted it during pregnancy and after menopause, when conception was not possible. Birth control as such is not mentioned in the Bible, but the Talmud lists exceptions when an "absorbent" could be used (by a minor, a pregnant woman, or a nursing wife—*b. Yebamoth* 100b). Generally the injunction to "be fruitful and multiply" prevailed (Gen. 1:28). One can appreciate how a tribe struggling to populate a country in which its people were outnumbered might value procreation highly, but such values are rendered questionable in a world facing uncontrolled overpopulation.

In addition, when a man acted like a woman sexually, male dignity was compromised. It was a degradation not only in regard to himself but for every other male. And the repugnance felt toward homosexuality was not just that it was deemed unnatural but also that it was considered alien behavior, representing yet one more incursion of pagan civilization into Israel's life. On top of that is the more universal repugnance heterosexuals tend to feel for acts and orientations foreign to them. (Left-handedness has evoked something of the same response in many cultures.)

Whatever the rationale for their formulation, however, the texts leave no room for maneuvering. Persons committing homosexual acts are to be executed. This is the unambiguous command of Scripture. The meaning is clear: anyone who wishes to base his or her beliefs on the witness of the Old Testament must be completely consistent and demand the death penalty for everyone who performs homosexual acts. (That may seem extreme, but there actually are some Christians urging this very thing today. It is unlikely, however, that any American court or religious body will condemn a homosexual to death, even though Scripture clearly commands it.)

For Christians, Old Testament texts have to be weighed against the New. Consequently, Paul's unambiguous con-

demnation of homosexual behavior in Rom. 1:26-27 must
be the centerpiece of any discussion.

> For this reason God gave them up to degrading passions.
> Their women exchanged natural intercourse for unnatural,
> and in the same way also the men, giving up natural inter-
> course with women, were consumed with passion for one
> another. Men committed shameless acts with men and
> received in their own persons the due penalty for their
> error.

No doubt Paul was unaware of the distinction between sexual orientation, over which one has apparently no choice,
and sexual behavior, over which one does. He seemed to
assume that those he condemned were heterosexuals who
were acting contrary to nature, "leaving," "giving up," or
"exchanging" their regular sexual orientation for that
which was foreign to them. Paul knew nothing of the modern psychosexual understanding of homosexuals as persons whose orientation is fixed early in life or perhaps even
genetically in some cases. For such persons, having heterosexual relations would be acting contrary to nature, "leaving," "giving up," or "exchanging" their natural sexual
orientation for one that was unnatural to them.

In other words, Paul really thought that those whose
behavior he condemned were "straight," and that they were
behaving in ways that were unnatural to them. Paul believed
that everyone was straight. He had no concept of homosexual orientation. The idea was not available in his world.
There are people who are genuinely homosexual by nature
(the exact cause no one really knows, and it is irrelevant). For
such a person it would be acting contrary to nature to have
sexual relations with a person of the opposite sex.

Likewise, the relationships Paul describes are heavy
with lust; they are not relationships between consenting
adults who are committed to each other as faithfully and
with as much integrity as any heterosexual couple. That
was something Paul simply could not envision. Some people assume today that venereal disease and AIDS are
divine punishment for homosexual behavior; we know it
as a risk involved in promiscuity of every stripe, homosex-

ual and heterosexual. In fact, the vast majority of people with AIDS the world around are heterosexuals; we can scarcely label AIDS a divine punishment.

And Paul believes that homosexual behavior is contrary to nature, whereas we have learned that it is manifested by a wide variety of species, especially (but not solely) under the pressure of overpopulation. It would appear then to be a quite natural mechanism for preserving species. We cannot, of course, decide human ethical conduct solely on the basis of animal behavior or the human sciences, but Paul here is arguing from nature, as he himself says, and new knowledge of what is "natural" is therefore relevant to the case.

Biblical Sexual Mores

Nevertheless, the Bible quite clearly takes a negative view of same-sex sexual relations, in those few instances where it is mentioned at all. But this conclusion does not solve the problem of how we are to interpret Scripture today. For there are other sexual attitudes, practices, and restrictions that are normative in Scripture but that we no longer accept as normative:

1. Old Testament law strictly forbids sexual intercourse during the seven days of the menstrual period (Lev. 18:19; 15:19-24), and anyone in violation was to be "extirpated" or "cut off from their people" (*kareth*, Lev. 18:29, a term referring to execution by stoning, burning, or strangling, or to flogging or expulsion; Lev. 15:24 omits this penalty). Today many people on occasion have intercourse during menstruation and think nothing of it. Should they be "extirpated"? The Bible says they should.

2. The punishment for adultery was death by stoning for both the man and the woman (Deut. 22:22), but here adultery is defined by the marital status of the woman. In the Old Testament, a man could not commit adultery against his own wife; he could only commit adultery against another man by sexually using the other's wife. And a bride who is found not to be a virgin is to be stoned to death (Deut.

22:13-21), but male virginity at marriage is never even mentioned. It is one of the curiosities of the current debate on sexuality that adultery, which creates far more social havoc, is considered less "sinful" than same-sex sexual relations. Perhaps this is because there are far more adulterers in our churches. Yet no one, to my knowledge, is calling for their stoning, despite the clear command of Scripture. And we ordain adulterers.

3. Nudity, a characteristic of paradise lost in the fall, was forbidden in Israel (2 Sam. 6:20; 10:4; Isa. 20:2-4; 47:3). When one of Noah's sons beheld his father naked, he was cursed (Gen. 9:20-27). To a great extent this nudity taboo probably even inhibited the sexual intimacy of husbands and wives. (This is still true of a surprising number of people reared in the Judeo-Christian tradition.) There were no doubt exceptions; the rabbis speak of nudity in the public baths, just as many of us grew up swimming nude at the old swimming hole. Attitudes vary widely, but we today are not so likely to regard what we believe to be appropriate nudity as a sin. The Bible itself is not of one mind on the subject; God apparently instigates the nakedness of Isaiah as a prophetic warning of approaching captivity (20:2-6).

4. Polygamy (many wives) and concubinage (a woman living with a man to whom she is not married) were regularly practiced in the Old Testament. Neither is ever condemned by the New Testament (with the questionable exceptions of 1 Tim. 3:2, 12 and Titus 1:6). Jesus' teaching about marital union in Mark 10:6-8 is no exception, since he quotes Gen. 2:24 as his authority (the man and the woman will become "one flesh"), and this text was never understood in Israel as excluding polygamy. A man could become "one flesh" with more than one woman, through the act of sexual intercourse. We know from Jewish sources that polygamy continued to be practiced within Judaism for centuries following the New Testament period. So if the Bible allowed polygamy and concubinage, why don't we?

5. A form of serial polygamy was the levirate marriage. When a married man in Israel died childless, his widow

was to have intercourse with his eldest brother. If he died without producing an heir, she turned to the next brother, and, if necessary, the next, and so on. Jesus mentions this custom without criticism (Mark 12:18-27 par.). Jews had virtually ceased to practice this custom by the time of Jesus, replacing it with the *halitzah* ceremony, which freed the woman from the obligation. I am not aware of any Christians who obey this unambiguous commandment of Scripture. Why do we ignore this law and yet preserve the ones regarding homosexual behavior?

6. The Old Testament nowhere explicitly prohibits sexual relations between unmarried consenting heterosexual adults, as long as the woman's economic value (bride price) is not compromised. (A Jewish girl came of age at twelve and a half, after which she assumed control from her father over her sexuality.) There are poems in the Song of Songs that eulogize a love affair between two unmarried persons, though commentators have often conspired to cover up the fact with heavy layers of allegorical interpretation. In various parts of the Christian world, quite different attitudes have prevailed about sexual intercourse before marriage. In some Christian communities, proof of fertility (that is, pregnancy) was required for marriage. This was especially the case in farming areas where the inability to produce children-workers could mean economic hardship. Today, many single adults, the widowed, and the divorced are reverting to "biblical" practice, while others believe that sexual intercourse belongs only within marriage. Which view is right?

7. The Bible virtually lacks terms for the sexual organs, being content with such euphemisms as "foot" or "thigh" for the genitals and using other euphemisms to describe coitus, such as "he knew her." Today most of us regard such language as "puritanical" or prudish, though as James Forbes notes in his introduction to this book, we in the church continue to show great reticence in public discussion of sex. But do we want to revert to biblical practice?

8. Semen and menstrual blood rendered all who touched them ritually unclean (Lev. 15:16-24). Intercourse rendered

one unclean until sundown; menstruation rendered the woman unclean for seven days. "Clean" and "unclean" do not refer to dirt but to a liminal state that recognizes the holiness of sex. Today most Christians treat semen and menstrual fluid from a completely secular point of view and regard them not as ritually "unclean" but only perhaps messy. In short, Christians no longer treat these fluids biblically.

9. Social regulations regarding adultery, incest, rape, and prostitution are, in the Old Testament, determined largely by considerations of the males' property rights over women. Prostitution was considered quite natural and necessary as a safeguard of the virginity of brides and the property rights of husbands (Gen. 38:12-19; Josh. 2:1-7). In later Jewish texts, a man was not guilty of sin for visiting a prostitute, though the prostitute (or maidservant) herself was regarded as a sinner. Paul must appeal to reason in attacking prostitution (1 Cor. 6:12-20); he cannot lump it in the category of adultery (v. 9). Today we are moving, with great social turbulence and at a high but necessary cost, toward a more equitable, nonpatriarchal set of social arrangements in which women are no longer regarded as the chattel of men. We are also trying to move beyond the double standard. Love, fidelity, and mutual respect replace property rights. We have, as yet, made very little progress in changing the double standard in regard to prostitution. As we leave behind patriarchal gender relations, what will we do with the patriarchalism in the Bible?

10. Israelites normally practiced endogamy—that is, marriage within the twelve tribes of Israel. There were exceptions, however. Joseph married the Egyptian Aseneth, Moses married Zipporah and the Cushite woman, Esther married Ahasueros. Until recently, endogamy prevailed in the American South, in laws against interracial marriage (miscegenation). We have witnessed, within the lifetime of many of us, the nonviolent struggle to nullify state laws against intermarriage and the gradual change in social attitudes toward interracial relationships. Sexual mores can alter quite radically even in a single lifetime.

11. The law of Moses allowed for divorce (Deut. 24:1-4); Jesus categorically forbids it (Mark 10:1-12; Matt. 19:9 softens his severity). Yet many Christians, in clear violation of a command of Jesus, have been divorced. Why, then, do some of these very people consider themselves eligible for baptism, church membership, communion, and ordination, but exclude gays and lesbians? What makes the one so much greater a sin than the other, especially considering the fact that Jesus never even mentioned homosexuality but explicitly condemned divorce? Yet we ordain and remarry people who have been divorced. Why not ordain and marry gays and lesbians?

12. The Old Testament regarded celibacy as abnormal, and 1 Tim. 4:1-3 calls compulsory celibacy a heresy. Other New Testament texts seem to support it (Matt. 19:10-12; 1 Cor. 7; Rev. 14:3-4; Acts 21:9; and Jesus' own example). The Catholic Church has made celibacy mandatory for priests and nuns. Some Christian ethicists demand celibacy of gays and lesbians, whether they have a vocation for celibacy or not. But this legislates celibacy by category, not by divine calling. Others argue that since God made men and women for each other in order to be fruitful and multiply, gay people reject God's intent in creation. But this would mean that childless couples, single persons, priests and nuns would be in violation of God's intention in their creation. Those who argue thus must explain why the apostle Paul never married. And are they prepared to charge Jesus with violating the will of God by remaining single? Certainly sexual relations between men and women are *normal*, else the race would die out. But they are not *normative*. God can bless the world through people who are married and through people who are single, and it is false to generalize from the marriage of most people to the marriage of everyone. In 1 Cor. 7:7 Paul goes so far as to call marriage a "charisma," or divine gift, to which not everyone is called. He preferred that people remain as he was—unmarried. In an age of overpopulation, perhaps same-sex orientation is especially sound ecologically!

13. In many other ways we have developed different norms from those explicitly laid down by the Bible. For example, "If men get into a fight with one another, and the wife of one intervenes to rescue her husband from the grip of his opponent by reaching out and seizing his genitals, you shall cut off her hand; show no pity" (Deut. 25:11f.). We, on the contrary, might very well applaud her for trying to save her husband's life!

14. The Old and New Testaments both regarded slavery as normal and nowhere categorically condemned it. Part of that heritage was the use of female slaves and captives as sexual objects, concubines, or involuntary wives by their male owners, which 2 Sam. 5:13, Judges 19-21 and Num. 31:18 sanctioned—and as many American slave owners did some 150 years ago, citing these and numerous other Scripture passages as their justification.

The point is not to ridicule Israel's sexual mores. Jews right up to the present have been struggling with the same interpretive task as Christians around issues of sexuality. The majority of U.S. Jewish groups (Reform, Conservative, and Reconstructionist) have gay-rights policies and have been involved in the same kinds of debates over homosexuality, masturbation, nonprocreative sexual intercourse, and so forth. The point is that both Jews and Christians must reinterpret the received tradition in order to permit it to speak to believers today.

The Problem of Authority

These cases are relevant to our attitude toward the authority of Scripture. They are not cultic prohibitions from the Holiness Code that have been set aside by Christians, such as rules about eating shellfish or wearing clothes made of two different materials. They are rules concerning sexual behavior, and they fall among the moral commandments of Scripture. Clearly we regard certain rules, especially in the Old Testament, as no longer binding. Other things we regard as binding, including legislation in the Old Testament that is not mentioned at all in the New. What is our principle of selection here?

For example, virtually all modern readers would agree with the Bible in rejecting:

- incest
- rape
- adultery
- intercourse with animals.

But we disagree with the Bible on most other sexual mores. The Bible condemned or discouraged the following behaviors which we generally allow:

- intercourse during menstruation
- celibacy (some texts)
- exogamy (marriage with non-Israelites)
- naming sexual organs
- nudity (under certain conditions)
- masturbation (some Christians still condemn this)
- birth control (some Christians still forbid this).

And the Bible regarded semen and menstrual blood as unclean, which most of us do not.

Likewise, the Bible permitted behaviors that we today condemn or have discontinued:

- prostitution
- polygamy
- levirate marriage
- sex with slaves
- concubinage
- treatment of women as property
- very early marriage (for the girl, age 11–13).

And while the Old Testament accepted divorce, Jesus forbade it. In short, of the sexual mores mentioned here, we agree with the Bible only on four of them, and disagree with it on sixteen!

Surely no Christians today would recommend reviving the levirate marriage. So why do we appeal to proof texts in Scripture in the case of homosexuality alone, when we feel perfectly free to disagree with Scripture regarding most other sexual practices? Obviously many of our choices in these matters are arbitrary. Mormon polygamy was outlawed in this country, despite the constitutional protection of freedom of religion, because it violated the sensibilities of the dominant Christian culture. Yet no explicit biblical prohibition against polygamy exists.

If we insist on placing ourselves under the old law, as Paul reminds us, we are obligated to keep every commandment of the law (Gal. 5:3). But if Christ is the end of the law (Rom. 10:4), if we have been discharged from the law to serve, not under the old written code but in the new life of the Spirit (Rom. 7:6), then all of these biblical sexual mores come under the authority of the Spirit. We cannot then take even what Paul himself says as a new Law. Christians reserve the right to pick and choose which sexual mores they will observe, though they seldom admit to doing just that. And this is as true of evangelicals and fundamentalists as it is of liberals and mainliners.

Judge for Yourselves

The crux of the matter, it seems to me, is simply that the Bible has no sexual ethic. Instead, it exhibits a variety of sexual mores, some of which changed over the thousand-year span of biblical history. Mores are unreflective customs accepted by a given community. Many of the practices that the Bible prohibits, we allow, and many that it allows, we prohibit. The Bible knows only a love ethic, which is constantly being brought to bear on whatever sexual mores are dominant in any given country, or culture, or period.

The very notion of a "sex ethic" reflects the materialism and splitness of modern life, in which we increasingly define our identity sexually. Sexuality cannot be separated from the rest of life. No sex act is "ethical" in and of itself, without reference to the rest of a person's life, the patterns of the culture, the special circumstances faced, and the will of God. What we have are simply sexual mores, which change sometimes with startling rapidity, creating bewildering dilemmas. Just within one lifetime we have witnessed the shift from the ideal of preserving one's virginity until marriage to couples living together for several years before getting married. The response of many Christians is merely to long for the hypocrisies of an earlier era.

I agree that rules and norms are necessary; that is what sexual mores are. But rules and norms also tend to be impressed into the service of the system of domination and to serve as a form of crowd control rather than to enhance the fullness of human potential. So we must critique the sexual mores of any given time and clime by the love ethic exemplified by Jesus. Such a love ethic is nonexploitative (hence no sexual exploitation of children, no using of another to his or her loss); it does not dominate (hence no patriarchal treatment of women as chattel); it is responsible, mutual, caring, and loving. Augustine already dealt with this in his inspired phrase, "Love God, and do as you please."

Our moral task, then, is to apply Jesus' love ethic to whatever sexual mores are prevalent in a given culture. This doesn't mean everything goes. It means that everything is to be critiqued by Jesus' love commandment. We might address younger teens, not with laws and commandments whose violation is a sin, but rather with the sad experiences of so many of our own children who find too much early sexual intimacy overwhelming and who react by voluntary celibacy and even the refusal to date. We can offer reasons, not empty and unenforceable orders. We can challenge both gays and straights to question their behaviors in the light of love and the requirements of fidelity, honesty, responsibility, and genuine concern for the best interests of the other and of society as a whole.

Christian morality, after all, is not an iron chastity belt for repressing urges, but a way of expressing the integrity of our relationship with God. It is the attempt to discover a manner of living that is consistent with who God created us to be. For those of same-sex orientation, as for heterosexuals, being moral means rejecting sexual mores that violate their own integrity and that of others, and attempting to discover what it would mean to live by the love ethic of Jesus.

Both Paul Egertson and Morton Kelsey argue that homosexual orientation has nothing to do with morality, any more than does left-handedness. It is simply the way some people are configured. Morality enters the picture when that predisposition is enacted. If we saw it as a God-given gift to those for whom it is normal, we could get beyond the acrimony and brutality that have so often characterized the unchristian behavior of Christians toward gays.

Approached from the point of view of love rather than that of law, the issue is at once transformed. Now the question is not "What is permitted?" but rather "What does it mean to love my gay neighbor?" Approached from the point of view of faith rather than works, the question ceases to be "What constitutes a breach of divine law in the sexual realm?" and becomes instead "What constitutes integrity before the God revealed in the cosmic lover, Jesus Christ?" Approached from the point of view of the Spirit rather than Christian legalism, the question ceases to be "What does Scripture command?" and becomes "What is the Word that the Spirit speaks to the churches now, in the light of Scripture, tradition, theology, and, yes, psychology, genetics, anthropology, and biology?" We can't continue to build ethics on the basis of bad science.

In a little-remembered statement, Jesus said, "Why do you not judge for yourselves what is right?" (Luke 12:57 NRSV). Such sovereign freedom strikes terror in the hearts of many Christians; they would rather be under law and be told what is right. Yet Paul himself echoes Jesus' sentiment when he says, "Do you not know that we are to judge angels? How much more, matters pertaining to this life!" (1 Cor. 6:3 RSV). The last thing Paul would want is for people to respond to his ethical advice as a new law engraved on tablets of stone. He himself is trying to "judge for himself what is right." If now new evidence is in on the phenomenon of homosexuality, are we not obligated—no, free—to reevaluate the whole issue in the light of all the available data and decide what is right, under God, for ourselves? Is this not the radical freedom for obedience in which the gospel establishes us?

Where the Bible mentions homosexual behavior at all, it clearly condemns it. I freely grant that. The issue is precisely whether that biblical judgment is correct. The Bible sanctioned slavery as well and nowhere attacked it as unjust. Are we prepared to argue today that slavery is biblically justified? One hundred and fifty years ago, when the debate over slavery was raging, the Bible seemed to be clearly on the slaveholders' side. Abolitionists were hardpressed to justify their opposition to slavery on biblical grounds. Yet today, if you were to ask Christians in the South whether the Bible sanctions slavery, virtually everyone would agree that it does not. In the same way, fifty years from now people will look back in wonder that the churches could be so obtuse and so resistant to the new thing the Holy Spirit was doing among us regarding homosexuality.

What happened to bring about such a monumental shift on the issue of slavery was that the churches were finally driven to penetrate beyond the legal tenor of Scripture to an even deeper tenor, articulated by Israel out of the experience of the Exodus and the prophets and brought to sublime embodiment in Jesus' identification with harlots, tax collectors, the diseased and maimed and outcast and poor. It is that God sides with the powerless. God liberates the oppressed. God suffers with the suffering and groans toward the reconciliation of all things. Therefore Jesus went out of his way to declare forgiven, and to reintegrate into society in all details, those who were identified as "sinners" by virtue of the accidents of birth, or biology, or economic desperation. In the light of that supernal compassion, whatever our position on gays, the gospel's imperative to love, care for, and be identified with their sufferings is unmistakably clear.

In the same way, women are pressing us to acknowledge the sexism and patriarchalism that pervades Scripture and has alienated so many women from the church. The way out, however, is not to deny the sexism in Scripture, but to develop an interpretive theory that judges even Scripture in the light of the revelation in Jesus. What Jesus gives us is a critique of domination in all its forms, a critique that can be turned on the Bible itself. The Bible thus contains the principles of its own correction. We are freed from bibliolatry, the worship of the Bible. It is restored to its proper place as witness to the Word of God. And that Word is a Person, not a book.

With the interpretive grid provided by a critique of domination, we are able to filter out the sexism, patriarchalism, violence, and homophobia that are very much a part of the Bible, thus liberating it to reveal to us in fresh ways the inbreaking, in our time, of God's domination-free order.

An Appeal for Tolerance

What most saddens me in this whole raucous debate in the churches is how sub-Christian most of it has been. It is characteristic of our time that the issues most difficult to assess, and which have generated the greatest degree of animosity, are issues on which the Bible can be interpreted as supporting either side. I am referring to abortion and homosexuality.

We need to take a few steps back and be honest with ourselves. I am deeply convinced of the rightness of what I have said in this essay. But I must acknowledge that it is not an airtight case. You can find weaknesses in it, just as I can in others' arguments. The truth is, we are not given unequivocal guidance in either area, abortion or homosexuality. Rather than tearing at each other's throats, therefore, we should humbly admit our limitations. How do I know I am correctly interpreting God's word for us today? How do you? Wouldn't it be wiser for Christians to lower the volume by 95 percent and quietly present our beliefs, knowing full well that we might be wrong?

I know of a couple, both well-known Christian authors in their own right, who have both spoken out on the issue of homosexuality. She supports gays and lesbians, passionately; he embraces them as persons but opposes their behavior. So far as I can tell, this couple still enjoy each other's company, eat at the same table, and, for all I know, sleep in the same bed.

We in the church need to get our priorities straight. We have not reached a consensus about who is right on the issue of homosexuality. But what is clear, utterly clear, is that we are commanded to love one another. Love not just our gay sisters and brothers who are often sitting beside us, acknowledged or not, in church, but all of us who are involved in this debate. These are issues about which we must painfully agree to disagree. Surely we don't have to tear whole denominations to shreds in order to air our differences on this point. If that couple I mentioned can continue to embrace across this divide, surely we can do so as well.

5

Biblical Fidelity and Sexual Orientation: Why the First Matters, Why the Second Doesn't

Ken Sehested

↙◑

Ken Sehested, executive director of the Baptist Peace Fellowship of North America (BPFNA) and editor of its quarterly journal, *Baptist Peacemaker,* was among the twenty-five American and Southern Baptists who founded the BPFNA in March 1984. Originally from West Texas and south Louisiana, Ken is a graduate of New York University and Union Theological Seminary, New York City. In 1995 the American Baptist Churches USA awarded him its highest honor, the Dahlberg Peace Award. That same year the Associated Church Press presented Ken its top magazine feature story award for his "Why I Am (Still) a Baptist," printed in the October 1994 issue of *The Witness,* an Episcopal magazine. Ken currently lives with his wife, Nancy Hastings Sehested, and two daughters, in the mountains of western North Carolina. In 1995 the Board of National Ministries of the American Baptist Churches USA, along with the Cooperative Baptist Fellowship (an alternative missions organization of Southern Baptist "moderates"), cut ties with the BPFNA following the organization's board statement on sexual orientation; later they reversed that decision.

↙◑

Culturally speaking, nothing seems to divide people more than the question of sexual orientation. At the center of this cultural wrestling match are the Christian churches. Much of the rationale for condemning homosexual behavior, even in secular institutions, is anchored in appeal to the Bible. Even the language of jurisprudence is affected by biblical tradition, with so-called sodomy laws criminalizing same-sex sexual relations.

We Baptists are on the verge of devouring ourselves in this dispute. But we're not alone: virtually every mainline Protestant body along with the Roman Catholic Church is embroiled in the controversy at the highest levels. Though the debate is less widespread within the "evangelical" end of the Protestant spectrum, the topic is sufficiently threatening to prompt preemptive maneuvers, as with the Southern Baptist Convention's recent constitutional amendment— the first in its 150-year history—prohibiting membership to congregations that condone homosexuality. (Voting "messengers" to the 1995 convention had to attest to that article of faith with their signature during registration.)

In the public arena, "the gay agenda" has replaced the "communist threat" as the battering ram of reactionary politics. Instead of a commie behind every bush, there's now a queer in every classroom, every congressional committee room, every battleship wardroom. Many have predicted that questions around sexual orientation will divide churches more severely than at any time since the debate over slavery a century and a half ago.

We find ourselves in the midst of a major public controversy. And my heart is heavier than it's ever been. Why such anxiety? There have been other controversies. We took a public stand against a very popular war in the Persian Gulf. We've engaged in acts of civil disobedience when convinced that holy obedience was at stake. There have been overseas trips involving a level of physical danger. So why the fearful heart now?

Because this subject is different. Simply raising the subject of homosexuality for discussion dredges up some of the most volatile passions in the human soul. Baptist journals that have rarely mentioned the Baptist Peace Fellowship of North America (BPFNA) in eleven years have recently devoted full editorials to our actions for gay and lesbian justice. Long-term friends threaten disaffiliation.

I've had nightmarish visions of eleven years of patient network-building run aground and splintered, not to mention ambitious new plans for the future. It's not so much the withdrawal of financial support that poses a danger. From the beginning, we chose to develop a financial base of member support rather than rely on institutional funding. More threatening is the prospect of losing the confidence of mainstream Baptist leaders around the world with whom we work.

Given the tension often accompanying the question of sexual orientation and the admittedly tenuous nature of our organization, it's fair to ask, "Why did the BPFNA board choose to wade into these troubled waters?" We have been interrogated both by those with principled convictions and by those with pragmatic considerations. The latter warn us that we can't take on every issue, that we will lose the solid core of our constituency for involvement on issues of broader consensus.

Each of these objections and a few more have been mental wrestling partners worthy of Jacob's angel at the Jabbok. Each has had not just one but several nights to work me over. Moreover, my personal passion rests in other arenas. Domestically, our cities are being wrecked by violence, often with racial overtones. Virtually every leading social indicator of human health in the African American community is lower now than when riots across the U.S. scorched our conscience a generation ago. Our addiction to guns needs attention from communities of faith. Fully one-fifth of U.S. children live in poverty. The struggle of Cuba to be free of U.S. imperial designs has a grip on my imagination. Additionally, we have privileged conversation with Baptists in a dozen countries involved in leadership to mediate civil strife and in movements of nonviolent resistance to injustice.

Isn't all this at risk when you address the question of justice in relation to sexual orientation? Yes. *Aren't you in danger of losing your credibility across the board for the sake of this one point of attention?* Could be. *And what about your efforts to show the connection between biblical faith and matters of justice and peace? Aren't you in danger of undermining that influence when you take a position in apparent opposition to that of the Bible?* That is a possibility.

Then why take the risk? Don't all these other involvements stretch your resources and threaten your existence enough, without adding the most volatile issue of all?

Why Take the Risk?

My response to this composite portrait of actual questions is three-fold. First, this is, simply, the right thing to do. Matters of justice cannot be segregated. Of course, we have to make choices, live within time and resource limitations. Often the hardest thing about our work is deciding what not to do, for there are so many points at which we could make a difference. Many of us, myself included, have resisted for too long speaking out on matters of simple human and civil rights for gay and lesbian people.

And while we can never be free of the need to make calculated choices, there comes a point when such calculation becomes compromise. After long hours of sometimes painful discussion, the BPFNA board has become convinced that the time for us is now. We hope our members and readers will join us in active and public opposition to gay-bashing—or at least not abandon our larger mission in disputing our discernment at this one point.

Second, we have a ready-made opportunity to practice our calling as reconcilers within our own household. Gay brothers and lesbian sisters are among our fellowship. We have listened to their stories. We know something of their pain. To continue formal silence in this regard would involve us in a profound level of hypocrisy.

Nonviolence is more than refusing to shoot someone. It is not to be confused with passivity or with sectarian withdrawal (in the name of moral purity). Rather it involves a commitment to willingly enter a situation of conflict, to absorb the assault (in this case, mostly of the verbal and emotional variety) without resort to revenge, to listen with empathy to the "enemy," which involves the willingness to have your mind changed. In occasions like ours, no amount of voting will bring healing. Parliamentary procedure must give way to the discipline of reconciliation.

Finally, there is no way to dodge the question of biblical authority. Although homophobia is a virulent force within the church as well as the larger culture, and although appeals to "biblical authority" often mask prejudice, there are those for whom genuine fidelity to Scripture is at stake. It also is for me.

What the Bible Does, and Does Not, Say

Homosexual behavior is mentioned in seven texts, four in Hebrew Scripture, three in the New Testament. The first text, Genesis 19, is the most common text of reference. It's the story of Sodom and Gomorrah, of Lot and the visit of the three angels.

The narrative is familiar. The angels approach Sodom, when they encounter Lot sitting in the gate of the city and accept his invitation of hospitality. After a meal, "the men of the city . . . both young and old, all the people to the last man" come banging on the door. The Sodomites demand to see the newly arrived guests, demanding to "know" them. Lot refuses, offering to send out his two virgin daughters instead. Just as the crowd gets unruly, the angels rescue Lot from their midst, shut the door, and strike the mob blind. Lot and his kin are commanded to leave immediately because of the impending destruction. They flee, instructed not to look back. Brimstone and fire rain over the cities. But in the escape, Lot's wife looks back and turns into a pillar of salt.

Three things are especially important here. First, Sodom and Gomorrah are already under sentence. In chapter 19, the heavenly messengers reveal that their mission is to destroy the cities. They want Abraham to know so that "he may charge his children and his household after him to keep the way of the Lord by doing righteousness and justice" (v. 19). The condemned cities obviously have not done so. Second, the context does make clear that the men of Sodom have sexual intentions with regard to the guests in Lot's house. But the intention is not so much homosexual activity as it is rape. And the principle impulse in rape—

whether homosexual or heterosexual—is not about sex. It is about power. Male rape of other males was a common form of humiliation and domination committed against defeated armies in the ancient world, as it is in modern prisons today.

Third, you would assume that if Sodom and Gomorrah's sin was homosexual relations, other authors in the Bible would make that connection. But nowhere does that happen! Listen to Ezekiel: "This was the guilt of your sister Sodom: she and her daughters had pride, excess of food, and prosperous ease, but did not aid the poor and needy. They were haughty and did abominable things before me" (16:49-50).

Amos warns that Israel will be overthrown just as God overthrew Sodom and Gomorrah (4:11) and for the same general reason: the poor are oppressed and the needy are crushed (4:1). Also in Isaiah: the people of Jerusalem and Judah "proclaim their sin like Sodom" (3:9). The charge? "Your hands are full of blood" (1:15); "the spoil of the poor is in your houses" and for "grinding the face of the poor" (3:14, 15). Indeed, "the daughters of Zion are haughty" and are "glancing wantonly with their eyes" (3:16). Also in Zephaniah: "Moab shall become like Sodom, and the Ammonites like Gomorrah" (2:9), for these have filled houses "with violence and fraud" (1:9).

The only New Testament reference to Sodom and Gomorrah comes from Jesus, who predicts a similar judgment in his own day (Matt. 10:14-15). Who will receive it, and why? Those towns that do not provide welcome and sustenance to his appointed missionaries who are to travel the countryside preaching and healing.

In all these references to the sin of Sodom and Gomorrah, the issue is wantonness. It is about domination of others, about malignant power, about God's intended shalom—harmony, right-relatedness. In each, God-relatedness and just relations among God's creatures are intimately linked. Spiritual realities and socioeconomic realities are mirror images.

The second pair of texts in the Old Testament that mention homosexual behavior, in Lev. 18:22 and 20:13, are nearly identical commands forbidding a man to lie with another man "as with a woman." Both judge such activity (as in Gen. 19) as an "abomination." Note here that the word *abomination* is not a moral or ethical term. Rather, it is always used to indicate a serious breach of ritual purity law. Other "abominations" before God include eating pork, misusing incense, and having intercourse during menstruation. These and many other prohibitions are connected to questions of what is clean and what is unclean in the eyes of God. The issue of clean and unclean becomes important in the final section of this article. The dilemma in making this Levitical text normative for faith is what we do with other prohibitions in this same material. Wearing garments made of two different materials is also prohibited, as are sowing a field with two kinds of seed, cutting one's hair where it meets the temple of a human face—among a host of other commands, commands that the church has never declared normative.

The remaining three biblical references to homosexual activity appear in the Pauline letters. The Gospels, oddly enough, are utterly silent on this point. "Sodomites" are mentioned in lists of "wrongdoers" (1 Cor. 6:9-10) and "the lawless and disobedient" (1 Tim. 1:9-10). In both these listings, however, there is considerable evidence that the language used indicates a condemnation of pederasty—the sexual and/or economic exploitation of children, particularly young boys—rather than against homosexual activity per se. In a similar way, Paul's description of women who "exchanged natural relations for unnatural" and of "men committing shameless acts with men" (Rom. 1:26-27) is set within a larger context of idolatry. Pagan temple cult prostitution, using adult men and women as well as young boys, was common in that day.

Even if you discount these contextual factors, even if you disregard all alternative explanations set out above, there's still a major issue of consistency in our notions of biblical authority. The preface for that issue has been mentioned: what about all those other prohibitions? The Bible prohibits gluttony at least as many times, even calling it a form of idolatry at one point (Phil. 3:19). According to some studies, 60 percent of the U.S. population is overweight, a percentage I would guess to be reflective of churchgoers. All but a tiny handful, who have biological disorders, are clearly gluttonous. Why not exclude these from our congregations? More caustic for us, especially us Baptists, is the Bible's repeated authorization of the institution of slavery. 1995 marked the 150th anniversary of the split among white Baptists in the U.S. over the issue of whether missionaries could also be slaveholders. It's right there in the Bible, in simple language: "Slaves, obey your masters" (Eph. 6:5).

The simple language of Scripture prohibits women from wearing gold jewelry, braiding their hair, and wearing expensive clothing (1 Pet. 3:3). In other words, gold wedding bands are a sign of apostasy! And not only are women to be silent in church (1 Cor. 14:34), but they also are to have their heads covered and their faces veiled (11:5-6).

Fasting is everywhere a discipline in Scripture, but almost never in our churches. Paul warned the church at Corinth to "not forbid speaking in tongues." Rarely is such behavior sanctioned in our churches. In that same letter, he urges the unmarried to remain that way, judging it "better." "Do not seek marriage" is his plain advice. (Except if you can't control your passion—implying that the New Testament foundation for marriage is uncontrollable sexual appetite.) He hedged on marriage, of course, noting, "I have no command of the Lord" (1 Cor. 7:25). Does that mean this part of Scripture is not divinely inspired? Taken together with Jesus' teaching that disciples will renounce biological family ties, where does this leave the "family values" movement?

The apparent disparity between biblical teaching on sexual morality and modern standards of church discipline is nowhere more evident than on the issue of divorce. Nowadays, divorce and remarriage are rarely cause for expulsion from the congregation. This is true even in the more morally-strict evangelical circles—even though Jesus clearly asserts the charge of adultery (Matt. 5:31-32, Luke 16:18, Mark 10:11-12).

The one time Jesus explicitly names the kinds of folk who are headed for eternal damnation, he lists only those who did not provide food for the hungry or drink for the thirsty, did not welcome strangers or provide clothing to the naked, did not visit prisoners. Maybe the Southern Baptist Convention should indicate that question on its messenger registration cards and ask for a signed attestation. These and dozens of other plain stipulations are routinely overlooked by even the most ardent defenders of biblical authority.

The interpretive layers in these questions are as subtle as they are many. I am convinced, however, that Scripture does have within its text an insight that helps us deal with these questions, a narrative relevant to questions of sexual orientation and biblical fidelity.

The Jerusalem Protocol

The story in Acts 10–15 is the narrative describing the struggle of the early Christian community as it moved from a parochial to a universal mission. The key characters of chapter 10 are Cornelius, a God-fearing Gentile, and Peter. First, Cornelius has a vision from God telling him to locate Peter. Peter likewise has a vision, of animals descending from heaven on a sheet. He is instructed to eat them; but they are unclean and compliance would be an "abomination" according to the Bible. His refusal is met with this rebuke: "What God has made clean, you must not call common or profane."

All of this is visionary preparation for Peter's being willing to commit an abomination—to associate with Cornelius, a profane, unclean Gentile who by definition is a religious pervert—at the prompting of a "holy angel," who is identified later in the chapter as the Holy Spirit.

In subsequent chapters this theological confusion over what is and is not the divinely inspired Word of God is eclipsed by a bevy of stories about the trials of early Christian missionary work: of the journeys of Paul and Barnabas, tales of persecution and imprisonment, the martyrdom of James. Chapter 15 hints at the coming doctrinal debate in the church with a report that certain Jewish Christians from Judea were insisting on the fundamentals of the faith: circumcision for the newly converted Gentile believers and, by implication, accountability to the law of Moses. They were insisting on the authority of the Bible.

Then comes the fight on the floor of the convention in Jerusalem. Missionary stories of revival breaking out among the (religiously perverted) Gentiles are told with jubilation. But some of the fundamentalists are upset that these converts are not being required to believe the Bible is literally true. The missionaries have gone soft on the "law of Moses."

The more conservative leaders argue that you either believe all of the Bible or none of it. Either it's authoritative or it's not. And the Bible (the "law of Moses") commands circumcision—the texts are plain, their meaning is indisputable.

Finally, Peter stood up and said, in effect: "I know what the Bible says. What I'm telling you is that I've seen indisputable evidence of the work of the Holy Spirit in the lives of these Gentile-perverts. God has cleansed their hearts by faith and has made no distinction between them and us. We don't exactly have a perfect track record when it comes to being faithful to the Bible ourselves."

Peter was onto something important. His was a precedent-setting theological argument: clear evidence of the presence of the Holy Spirit—evidence attested to in the Bible—overrules any particular regulation. The regulations, in other words, are in service to the Spirit, not the other way around. I call it the "Jerusalem Protocol." The idea is ancient and deeply biblical: "The only thing that counts is faith working through love," according to Paul (Gal. 5:6). Fidelity to the Bible, to paraphrase Jesus, can be summarized in two intertwined statements: "You shall love the Lord your God with all your heart, and with all your soul, and with all your mind" and "your neighbor as yourself" (Matt. 22:37-40).

Is homosexuality compatible with Christian faith? Is heterosexuality compatible with Christian faith? Uncircumcised or circumcised? None of these questions, I would suggest, is relevant. To quote sacred Scripture, "We believe that we will be saved through the grace of the Lord Jesus, just as they will" (Acts 15:11).

Part Three

~

What Are the Issues?

6

Homosexualities

Morton Kelsey and Barbara Kelsey

◠

Morton Kelsey is an Episcopal priest, marriage and family counselor, and professor emeritus of Notre Dame University. One of today's most important religious writers and a popular lecturer and retreat leader, Kelsey has consistently been in the forefront, defining issues long before they emerged as critical for the life of the churches. His book *Tongue Speaking: The History and Meaning of Charismatic Experience* was one of the first published discussions of what was to become a contentious theme among Christians. He was one of the first to make the spiritual contribution of Jung's psychology available to American Christians. He is the author of more than twenty-five books, including the best-selling *Dreams: A Way to Listen to God, The Other Side of Silence: A Guide to Christian Meditation,* and *Christo-Psychology.* Barbara Kelsey is a counselor and teacher of the Myers-Briggs personality inventory. The following is adapted from *Sacrament of Sexuality* (Warwick, N.Y.: Amity House, 1986), 32–35, 183, 192.

◠

Five overlapping but different common sexual adaptations are found among human beings—heterosexual, homosexual, bisexual, celibate, and asexual. And there are many variations in each of these adaptations. As Kinsey pointed out, we should speak of heterosexualities, homosexualities, bisexualities, celibacies, asexualities. Using the singular is very misleading. Of course these are not entirely distinct and separable categories; they are more like concentrations of points on a many-pointed scale. Certainly we need to recognize that there may be parts of our lives in each category; we are very complicated creatures. However, children, as they mature, usually adopt one of these basic orientations. Part of our sexual identity is a willed decision

or choice about what our behavior will be. Sometimes physiological and psychological factors override these decisions.

People with a heterosexual identity will find themselves
primarily attracted to people of the opposite sex for their
sexual gratification. They see themselves as males or
females and find themselves sexually drawn to their oppo-
sites. The continuance of the species depends upon this
attraction, and it is deeply rooted in our biological makeup.
This does not mean that people with this identity may not
occasionally feel some attraction to those of the same sex.
Heterosexuality expresses itself in many different ways.

Human sexual feelings are not entirely determined by
the procreative drive, for men and women can be exclu-
sively attracted to the same sex for their sexual satisfaction
and for experience of erotic intimacy. The words *homosexual*
and *homoerotic* are derived from Greek words meaning
attraction to the same sex. There are as many different
kinds of homosexual relationships as there are heterosexual.
They range from permanent, deeply caring unions to short-
term relationships, to one-night stands, to rape. American
society puts many roadblocks in the way of the more permanent kind of sexual relationships between people of the
same sex.

Those with a bisexual orientation (and surveys show far
more in this range than is ordinarily believed) have strong
or moderate attractions sexually and emotionally toward
both sexes. People in this position may be in long-term relationships with people of the same sex or people of the
opposite sex. They may live a single lifestyle with sexual
experiences with both sexes, or, like people of any orientation, they may opt for celibacy. Some human beings are able
to have warm, caring sexual relations with both sexes. The
person with this orientation is often forced to face two different and seemingly opposed aspects of his or her inner
life and can be driven to despair. But if the person can stand
this tension, he or she may find an inner wholeness. Society
offers little direction or help for bisexual people, and there
are very few support groups available for them such as

have recently developed for those with a primarily homosexual orientation.

Most of us usually think in terms of either/or distinctions rather than a many-pointed scale. One of the most important findings of Kinsey and his associates related to sexual behavior in regard to the three categories just mentioned. They presented a scale showing how exclusive heterosexuality shaded into bisexuality and finally to exclusive homosexuality.

Less than 50 percent of the male population surveyed could claim that their sexual experience was totally heterosexual (and less than that if childhood sexual play was considered). Among women less than 60 percent could make that claim. On the other hand, exclusive homosexual activity varied from 1 to 3 percent among women and 3 to 16 percent among men.

There are few subjects about which there is more general prejudice and lack of information than homosexuality; comparable in intensity are the violence of race prejudice and the popular attitudes toward mental illness and mental institutions that existed at the turn of the century. Yet homosexuality is far from rare. Margaret Mead has pointed out that almost all cultures of the world show some evidence of homosexual practice and that in a number of these cultures homosexual orientation earns a person honor and veneration. Mircea Eliade in his definitive book *Shamanism* showed that many of the shamans, both male and female, have this orientation. And an exhaustive cross-cultural study concludes that 64 percent of the 76 societies investigated permitted homosexuality. In the other 36 percent of the societies, although homosexual actions were prohibited and punished with varying degrees of severity, they were still clandestinely present.

We do not look upon homosexuality as a neurotic problem, but as a basic personality pattern, over which individuals have little control. Homosexuality is not something that should be changed or treated punitively; rather, it should be understood in a psychological and physiological context.

The goal is to cease seeking wholeness in and through another person, to cease using another person, no matter what his or her sexual orientation, just for personal fulfillment. To come to potential wholeness we must find ourselves in these relationships and bring the various different and sometimes warring parts of ourselves before God. Then the Divine Lover may fashion a unity within us and enable us to go back into relationships with human beings more interested in giving than in receiving, in loving than in being loved. Such wholeness doesn't come easily; it is the result of a lifetime of work and struggle.

7

Accepting What Cannot Be Changed

David G. Myers

～っ

Hope College (Michigan) social psychologist David Myers is an award-winning researcher and teacher and the author of psychology's most widely studied text, *Psychology*. His scientific research, supported by National Science Foundation grants and fellowships, has appeared in two dozen periodicals, including *Science* and *American Scientist*. Myers also has digested psychological research for the lay public in ten books and through articles in more than two dozen magazines, from *Scientific American* to *Christian Century*. In *The Pursuit of Happiness: Who Is Happy— and Why* (1993), he challenged America's individualism and materialism and affirmed the significance of positive traits, committed relationships, and religious faith. He has written five books that relate psychological research to Christian faith (most recently, *Psychology through the Eyes of Faith*). Myers has served as an elder in both the Presbyterian Church and the Reformed Church in America. He and his wife, Carol, are parents of three grown children.

～っ

As a family advocate, I have written of the corrosive effects of pornography, teen sexual activity, and family disintegration. I have spoken and written on "America's social recession." And I am supporting a new citizen movement that aims to renew the moral roots of civilized society. So I share many of the family-values concerns of fellow Christians.

Why, then, are increasing numbers of folks like me (and even some conservatives such as William Bennett) now persuaded that gay rights pose little or no threat to family values? For three reasons:

1. *The Bible has little to say about homosexuality.* Many of us Christians have awakened to how mute the Bible is regarding

a committed homosexual union between mature adults. The Bible's mere seven mentions of homosexual behavior—what gay Christians have called "the clobber passages"—include some lines of the Leviticus purity code (which includes many behavioral rules from which Jesus liberates us), some sentences in Corinthians and Timothy that many biblical Greek scholars say referred to men exploiting boys, and a debated passage in Romans. Although Jesus affirmed marriage, he spoke no recorded words about homosexual behavior (though he had much to say about the poor and powerless). At the very least, it wasn't a big issue for the biblical writers.

2. *Today's greater tolerance seems not to have amplified homosexuality.* Gays and lesbians are a small minority—perhaps 2 or 3 percent of the population, according to some studies—and their numbers appear not to have grown with their coming out or with the passage of gay rights laws. Contrary to the concern that gay role models would entice more people into homosexuality, all the available surveys show no increase in the gay minority.

3. *Sexual orientation appears not to be a choice.* If you are heterosexual, can you recall a time when you *chose* to be so? Nearly all of us say no—it's just the way we are. So why are some people gay, others straight? Some answers:

- There is no known parental or psychological influence on sexual orientation. We have learned that factors once believed crucial actually don't matter. Sexual orientation appears not to be influenced by social example, overprotective mothering, or child abuse. If some new parents were to seek my advice on how to influence the sexual orientation of their newborn, I could only say, after a half century of research, that we're utterly clueless. So far as I know, there is nothing you can do. Nor does it seem to matter who your child's gym or English teacher is.
- Biological factors are more and more looking important. Although this scientific story is still being written, we have learned that siblings of gays and lesbians, especially their identical twins, are more likely than

people without close gay relatives to be gay themselves. Genetic instructions must be manifest in physiology. So it shouldn't surprise us that new evidence points to both prenatal hormonal differences and brain differences in a region known to influence sexual behavior. One recently published scientific review concludes that "the emerging neuroanatomical picture is that, in some brain areas, homosexual men are more likely to have female-typical neuroanatomy than are heterosexual men."[1] A brand-new report suggests that this female-typical pattern extends to a prenatally-influenced fingerprint difference between gay and straight men.[2] If, as it's beginning to look, sexual biology is destiny, than why not (regardless of our views) spend our energies where they can make a difference—on the real problems of a culture in social decline?

- Efforts to change one's sexual orientation usually (some say always) fail. People who have experimented with homosexual behavior (as many heterosexual people do) can turn away from it. And homosexuals, like heterosexuals, can become celibate. But a recent review of research on efforts to help people change their sexual orientation concludes that there is "no evidence indicating that such treatments are effective."[3] Christian ex-gay organizations have had a go at this. But most are now either defunct or abandoned by their ex-ex-gay founders. Reading their literature, one is struck by the admitted homosexual temptations many "ex-gays" still struggle with.

Isn't it therefore wiser for us all to relax—and to enjoy God's acceptance "just as I am?" Can we not accept our own and others' sexual orientation without excusing promiscuity, exploitation, or self-destructive behavior? Straight or gay, we all face moral choices over options that include abstinence and long-term commitment.

Everywhere our culture seems preoccupied with the "homosexual threat to family values." As one who is terribly concerned with the corrosion of family values, I am reminded of C. S. Lewis's tongue-in-cheek advice from senior devil Screwtape to his apprentice devil—corrupt by diverting their attention: "The game is to have them all running about with fire extinguishers whenever there is a flood."

Could it be that those who use the anti-gay agenda to divert us from a focus on the family and from the declining well-being of America's children and youth are unwittingly heeding Screwtape's advice?

1. Gladue, B. A. "The Biopsychology of Sexual Orientation" in *Current Directions in Psychological Science* 3 (1994) 150–54.

2. Hall, J. A. Y. and Kimura, D. "Dermatoglyphic Assymetry and Sexual Orientation in Men" in *Behavioral Science* 108 (1994) 1203–6.

3. Haldeman, D. C. "The Practice and Ethics of Sexual Orientation Conversion Therapy" in *Journal of Consulting and Clinical Psychology* 62 (1994) 221–27.

8

Homosexuality: A Word Not Written

Maria Harris and Gabriel Moran

Maria Harris and Gabriel Moran are internationally known and traveled theologians and Christian educators. Maria has taught at New York, Fordham, and John Carroll Universities as well as Andover Newton and Auburn Theological Seminaries. She has served as an editor for *PACE* (Professional Approaches for Christian Educators), book review editor for the journal *Religious Education,* and president of the Association of Professors and Researchers of Religious Education (APRRE). Among her eighty-five articles and twelve books are *Proclaim Jubilee* (1996), *Jubilee Time* (1995), and *Dance of the Spirit* (1991). Gabriel Moran teaches in the Department of Culture and Communication at New York University and directs the doctoral program in religious education there. He has also taught at Manhattan College, New York Theological Seminary, Boston College, and elsewhere. He too has served as president of APRRE. In his career he has published more than two hundred articles and seventeen books, including *Showing How: The Act of Teaching* (1997), *Uniqueness* (1992), and *No Ladder to the Sky* (1987). Together this couple has had a major impact in reshaping the field of religious education.

Can something be condemned if the word for that something does not exist? The same question can be asked about approving something, but more often the question concerns something that is thought to be deserving of condemnation. The question takes on special importance where there is an authoritative text from the past. Although the Bible and the Qur'an are perhaps the most representative examples of such texts, they are not alone. The United States Constitution is regularly invoked for approval or disapproval of realities that the writers of the document could not have had in mind. The twentieth-century Supreme Court

ruled that "separate but equal education" is unconstitu-
tional while a "right to privacy" is constitutionally protect-
ed. A historian would find it difficult to say which
respective words in the United States Constitution disavow
one practice and support the other. In the case of the Constitution, the Supreme Court becomes the bridge between
past text and present realities, even though this function of
the Court is itself not clearly stated in the Constitution.

For a Christian, the Bible is not just a document of gov-
ernmental principles. Its importance to Christian life is
greater than is the Constitution for citizens of the United
States. The Bible is believed to be a complete guide to life; its
importance is based on the belief that it is *inspired* by God.
(The belief of Muslims that the Qur'an is *revealed* by God
raises different issues that cannot be explored here.) Christian communities and people who consider themselves
Christian tend to believe strongly in living in accord with
the Christian Bible.

Anything that is condemned in the Christian Bible cannot
be accepted as part of a Christian way of life. Idolatry, incest,
and murder are clear-cut examples of unacceptable behavior.
Despite the vast changes over the millennia, there is continuity in the meaning of the original terms and their translation
into modern languages. In the opposite direction, the Bible's
approval of the love of neighbor, compassion for the suffering, and the restoration of stolen goods are also names of
activities that are translatable without major problems.

Beyond a small number of clear commands that refer to
specific actions (the New Testament actually has very few of
these), most Christians recognize the need for interpretive
help in understanding the Bible. Are "human rights" something to be approved? The Bible does not have the term to
ask the question. Should the Christian church be democratic? An answer presupposes both an interpretation of biblical
texts and an agreed-upon meaning of the contemporary
term *democratic*.

There is a way of reading the Bible that, while called "lit-
eral," is actually a disregarding of the *words* for the sake of

ideas. That is, a set of ideas is assumed to be immutable so that the words are mere labels. The nonexistence of a term is not taken seriously; the reality, it is assumed, was condemned *in other words*. "Homosexuality" is an interesting example of what is supposedly condemned by the Bible in a few texts. One of the "proof texts" is in the Book of Leviticus: "You shall not lie with a male as with a woman; it is an abomination" (18:22). The practice of a contemporary Christian scanning the Book of Leviticus to decide what is approved or disapproved in contemporary life is itself an intriguing image. Paul's view, however, is undeniably central for a Christian. The person who assumes Paul condemned homosexuality thinks it is obvious that he had the same idea in mind as the contemporary reader. The fact that the term *homosexual* was invented in the nineteenth century is not considered relevant. But we return to our opening question: Can you condemn something which you do not have a word for? How exactly is the condemnation to be stated?

There is no denying that at least one writer of the New Testament, Paul in his Epistle to the Romans, condemned certain sexual practices that he thought were perversions. "Men committed shameless acts with men" (Rom. 1:27). But should what he condemned be given the name "homosexuality"? At the least, it is anachronistic to impose a modern word on an ancient document. For example, one might wish to argue that the roots of modern anti-Semitism go back to the New Testament. But to say that the New Testament is "anti-Semitic" is to apply a modern word (coincidentally invented at almost the same moment as *homosexual*) with a range of meaning unintelligible for the New Testament era. But is not *homosexual* a simple idea that anyone can identify? Does not everyone today know exactly what is being referred to? Would not St. Paul's reaction to hearing the word for the first time be, "That is just what I mean"?

In 1994, Stephen Donaldson, the president of "Stop Prisoner Rape," wrote a letter to the editor in *The New York*

Times. He pointed out that the *Times* had referred to the prevalence in our prisons of "homosexual rape." Donaldson pointed out that practically all rape in prisons is "heterosexual." Which is correct? If one means by "homosexual" a certain set of behaviors between people of the same sex, then prison rape is "homosexual." However, if one means by "homosexual" a person's fundamental orientation in sexual life, then prison rape is seldom "homosexual." Can anyone say which is the correct usage? Although both meanings are present in ordinary speech, the *Times* in this case would seem to have badly faltered. If one accepts the existence of people with a homosexual orientation, then the characterization of prison rape as "homosexual" becomes misleading and offensive.

The ambiguity still present today in the term *homosexual* reflects the evolution in its meaning since its invention a century and a quarter ago. Invented as a name for either a disease or a crime, *homosexual* was nonetheless available when the twentieth century distinguished between sexual behavior and sexual "orientation," a distinction that has been the basis of political tolerance. Many religious groups can support the civil rights of gay and lesbian people while not approving same-sex sexual relations. Whether such a policy can be consistently maintained on a long-term basis is doubtful, but the recognition of persons with civil rights is a big step. The term *homosexual* remains ambiguous today. But when someone is said to be "a homosexual," the presumption today is most likely to be that a person is homosexually oriented, whether or not this person has ever engaged in sexual relations with a member of the same sex.

At midcentury, when Alfred Kinsey did his study of male sexuality, he distinguished between 40 percent of the population who had engaged in "homosexual experiences" and the 5 to 10 percent who were "genuinely homosexual," that is, whose primary orientation was toward same-sex love. Experience of sexual activity between two males could range from innocent experimentation to predatory violence to deeply committed love. What emerged for some of Kinsey's subjects, and perhaps more clearly for some men today, is that their sexual lives are oriented to same-sex love.

What does the Christian Bible say of such men and their female counterparts? Nothing directly. No judgment is made about gay and lesbian people; the question could not be asked, because the language was not available to do the asking. That is not to say that the Christian Bible offers no guidance to persons who have a same-sex orientation. Starting from the first chapter of Genesis, the Bible affirms that all creation is good because it is the work of God. The Bible also warns that all human desire can go astray and become corruptive. Sexual desire is especially dangerous not because it is evil but because it is so important a human good. Sexual life needs regulation because it is integral to the community's present existence and the foundation of its continuance into the future.

For most of human history, the sexual life of humans, like that of other animals, was immediately related to the reproduction of offspring. The nearly exponential growth of the population in the twentieth century has made both possible and necessary the exploration of human sexuality as a reality of its own. (It might be noted that although Jewish attitudes toward sexuality have generally been more positive than many Christian groups, the Jewish attitude toward homosexuality is influenced by the precariously low reproductive rate in the Jewish community.)

At the end of the twentieth century, individuals are probably no wiser than they ever have been about their sexual lives, but the human race undeniably has a different understanding of sexuality from what it had in the past. Studies subsequent to the two Kinsey Reports have confirmed the fact that the human race has an imaginative diversity of sexual expression. Sexual intimacy between consenting partners of the same sex seems to be nothing less and nothing more than part of that wonderful range of expression.

What would Paul make of today's sexual scene? It really is not possible to lift people out of one place in history and situate them in another. Presumably they could learn the language of a new era if given time to adjust. We can also speculate on the presumptive continuity of their personalities and the consistency in their judgments. Paul, one could guess, would be skeptical of aspects of gay and lesbian culture, as he was skeptical of a wide variety of sexual practices in the first century. But having done some reading on homosexuality, he would presumably not be so shocked by practices that he encountered in the Greek culture of his time.

A Christian today might even think that Paul would see homosexuality as part of God's creation, sanctified by the Incarnation. The world of our bodily senses is not a veil that obscures divinity. The material world, whatever its groans and travails, is the expression of divine goodness. The best impulses of that world—the genuine struggles for the fulfillment of bodily existence—cannot be dismissed. We human beings are often confused as to what impulses are "best" and which struggles are "genuine." However, that uncertainty is a call to listen more attentively, study more diligently, and choose more carefully. We do that as Christians in the light of the whole New Testament, which is mainly about the struggle for justice and the need for love. People's sexual expressions have to be seen within that context.

9

Exploring the Morality of Homosexuality

Lewis B. Smedes

～

Lew Smedes taught theology and ethics at Fuller Theological Seminary in Pasadena for twenty-eight years until his retirement four years ago. He has been married for almost fifty years—quite an accomplishment, he quips, for his wife. In addition to his stint at Fuller, he has taught at Calvin College and the Free University of Amsterdam. Among his many published titles are *Shame and Grace* (1993), *A Pretty Good Person* (1990), *Caring and Commitment* (1988), and *Mere Morality: What God Expects from Ordinary People* (1983). The following is adapted from *Sex for Christians: The Limits and Liberties of Sexual Living*, rev. ed. (Eerdmans, 1994), 238–44.

～

Homosexuality is a mystery. But then heterosexuality is a mystery too. So why should we expect homosexuality to be simple?

Another mystery is why heterosexual people get as fevered as they do about homosexuality. It is certainly appropriate for heterosexuals to size up homosexual behavior from a moral point of view. But why the furious fuss that many heterosexuals create when they aim their moral guns on gays and lesbians?

What danger to straight people is posed by homosexuals? Some say that they are a threat to the family, but none tells us how. Some fear they might abuse our children, but no facts have ever been adduced to show that they are anymore likely to do so than heterosexual people are. Do homosexuals threaten to invade our homes, steal our property, rape our daughters? What we know is that homosexual men are murdered by heterosexual people just for being gay;

what we also know is that there is no record of a heterosexual being murdered for not being gay. Why, then, I wonder, in a world of violence, starving children, cruel tyrannies, and natural disasters, are Christian people so steamed up about the harmless and often beneficent presence of gays and lesbians among us?

Reading the creation stories and what the New Testament tells us about marriage and family persuades me that the Creator originally intended the human family to flourish through heterosexual love. But nature has gone awry, as it sometimes does; and it seems most reasonable to me to believe that God intends homosexual people to bear their destined burden in as morally responsible a way as they can. And I further believe that a committed partnership of love is one morally responsible way to do so.

My Evangelical friends would respond to this by reminding me that what I believe is not really important; the question is: What does the Bible say? My answer is that, as far as I can tell, the New Testament gives no special or specific guidance about the moral choices that gay people should make. Further, in view of how assured many evangelicals are that the Bible condemns such partnerships as I approve of, it seems important to me to consider some aspects of homosexuality that the Bible *does not say* anything about. So I shall spend the rest of this essay talking about a telling assortment of things homosexual that the Bible is silent about.

The Bible does not tell us anything about a condition called homosexuality. The Bible observes that certain males were making love with other males. And females were making love with females. It tells us God did not approve of what they were doing. Probably the biblical writers assumed that these people were heterosexual people who were acting contrary to their own normal inclinations. The writers do not appear to have known anything about *a human condition called homosexuality.* That is, they do not even consider the possibility that a male, for example, may be disposed toward love for other males, disposed from before birth, disposed in the depths of his very being.

The Bible does not tell us how people get to be homosexual people. Scientific research offers evidence that some people are genetically disposed toward homosexuality. It is bred in their bones, set before they were born, in the way it is decided that they will be boys or girls. Not everyone accepts the evidence for a genetic cause. Many still hold that early childhood experiences influence sexual orientation. But whatever the link between genes and environment, gays and lesbians did not choose to be what they are. They only discovered what they had always been. And, for most of them, their discovery brought them more than their share of fear and shame. Indeed, many, if not most, would have given almost anything they had if giving it could have changed them.

Thus it seems clear that gays and lesbians are no more responsible for being homosexual than I am for being heterosexual. And therefore God does not judge them for being homosexual any more than God rewards me for being heterosexual.

The Bible does not tell us whether homosexuality is "curable." With God all things are possible, but even with God not everything is likely. God does not do everything it is possible for God to do. I know gay people who have prayed for change with all their hearts' passion. They have linked up with charismatic healers and exorcists. They have spent thousands on therapy. But though they may have changed in many healthy ways, they did not move an inch away from their homosexual base. When they prayed, they received the same answer Paul got when he prayed for God to remove his thorn: "My grace will be enough for you."

The Bible does not tell us about the sorts of persons homosexual people are likely to be. The Bible (Rom. 1:26-27) tells us that

God at one time permitted certain ungrateful heterosexual people to lapse into homosexual behavior. But it does not speak about the sorts of people that gays and lesbians are.

The Bible does not tell us about the character of gay people as a special class, any more than it tells me about the character of my fellow Dutchmen. It tells us only that we all have fallen short on character and that Christ died for the likes of us all. All I know about gays and lesbians is what I discern them to be as friends and neighbors and fellow Christians. What I have discerned from knowing them is that gay people are as likely to be honest and courageous and loving as any other class of people is. They are as likely to love God and seek God's will and mercy as any heterosexual is.

The Bible tells us that homosexual behavior is unnatural, but does not explain why it is unnatural. To many of us, "unnatural" suggests something ugly and abhorrent and certainly nothing that should be encouraged. This, they believe, is what St. Paul must have meant by "unnatural." But, one asks, is this also what he meant when he said that it is contrary to nature for a man to wear long hair (1 Cor. 11:14) and for women to curl their hair or pray without a veil (1 Cor. 11:6, 13). If it is, then most of us have a depraved sense of proper tonsorial styling.

What, then, makes homosexuality "unnatural"? Traditional Christian moralists believed that natural sex was the sort that could produce children and thus keep the human family in business. Homosexuality, on the other hand, has a built-in baby-making deficiency, and this made it not only abhorrent but dangerous as well.

Not many modern Christians, at least not many Protestant Christians, hold this traditional view anymore. Most of us believe that human sex is natural when it expresses intimate, personal, and committed love. For moderns, producing children may be a serendipitous by-product, if desired, but not the teleological end of sexuality. What they do not always see clearly is that their new view of natural sex pulls the rug from under their most fervent moral judgment against homosexuality.

I, on the other hand, happen to be a traditionalist; I do believe that having babies is the teleological bent of sexuality. And my traditionalism leads me to suppose that homosexuality is a product of nature sometimes gone awry. But this, in turn, leads me to assume that God wants gay people to make the best life they can within the limits of what errant nature gives them. I think that creating families by adopting babies is a parallel. It does not fit the Creator's original design, and, in that sense, my family of three adopted children is not "natural." But it seems to me that creating families through adoption is a way that God honors and blesses. Would not God also see same-sex partnerships as a morally worthy improvisation on the "unnatural"?

The Bible does not tell us about the personal quality of homosexual relationships. Paul tells us in the first chapter of Romans that God abandoned certain people to their lusts as punishment for their ingratitude. Some people conclude from this that what passes as same-sex love is a false front for a whirlpool of lust.

But anyone who knows gays and lesbians knows that they love each other as spiritually and nobly as heterosexual people love each other. Listen to the loving longing of one celibate gay Christian man for a person he loves: "My mind, my affection fastens on . . . the loveliness of his character and the beauty of his form. . . . My love is clean and noble. Why may I not live with him as my other?" Does this man's longing smack of brute lust?

These, then, are some things the Bible does *not* tell us about homosexuality. What, then, should we think about the morality of homosexual behavior in the light of what the Bible does say and in the light of what we can discern in the lives of real people? Here is a summary of what I think:

- I think that gays and lesbians are not responsible for their sexual orientation toward loving people of their own gender.
- I think that, as a class, homosexual people are as moral, as spiritual, as decent and good, as creative,

and as much in need of the grace of God as heterosexual people are.

- I think that there is a measure of tragedy in homosexuality and that gays and lesbians bear the burden of living as morally within their limits as the rest of us are called to live within the limits of whatever tragedy may be ours.
- I think that gays and lesbians, like the rest of us, are called to achieve the best moral relationships of love that are possible for them within the limits of a condition they did not choose.
- I think that gays and lesbians merit the same rights and bear the same responsibilities within society that anyone else does.
- I think that, if celibacy is not possible, it is better for gays and lesbians to live together in committed monogamous relationships of love than not. Same-sex partnerships that are committed offer the best moral option available.

These are some things I have come to believe after studying the Holy Scripture, after reflecting on Christian tradition, and after trying to enrich my knowledge and discernment with the insight of love. I may be wrong. I may not be seeing reality as clearly as I think I am. I am willing to learn from those who are willing to share their discernment with me. But this is what I believe.

Part Four

~

Assessing Christian Tradition

10

Where the Gospel Leads Us

Richard Rohr, OFM

◢◣

Father Richard Rohr is a Franciscan of the New Mexico Province. He was the founder and for thirteen years the pastor of the New Jerusalem Community in Cincinnati, Ohio, followed by eight years as animator of the Center for Action and Contemplation in Albuquerque, New Mexico. Richard now lives in a Franciscan community and divides his public time between local work and preaching and teaching around the world. He is probably best known for his audio- and videotapes. Among his publications are *Jesus' Plan for a New World* (1996) and *Job and the Mystery of Suffering* (1996). He is internationally known for *Discovering the Enneagram* with Andreas Ebert (1990), and *Enneagram II: Advancing Spiritual Discernment* (1995). He lectures frequently on men's spirituality, community building, and, above all, the integration of action and contemplation, which he perceives to be the most critical theological issue facing practicing Christians today.

◢◣

It is time to faithfully address the issue of homosexuality. I have talked about it on many of my tapes over the years, and my belief has not changed. I think God would ask of the homosexual relationship exactly what God asks of the heterosexual relationship: truth, faithfulness, long-suffering, and the continuing forgiveness of the other. "Against these there is no law!" (Gal. 5:23). It's amazing how we are willing to avoid modeling and living these demanding virtues in favor of judgments about mere physicality that we can more easily measure, punish, and mandate. As others have said, the church continually slips into "spiritual materialism" while calling materialism a sin in others.

The Achilles' heel of the official Catholic position is necessitated by its own theology. Cardinal Ratzinger says that we do not consider the state of homosexuality a sin (this is actually quite an advancement in our thinking and implies that homosexuality is probably seen as an unchosen condition), but only "acting" accordingly. Apart from the inconsistency with the theory of "natural law" (things must act according to their nature), this thinking proposes a second impossibility—to "mandate" a charism which is by definition a *free* gift. You cannot possibly order someone to have a charism, the "gift" of celibacy for example. It is an oxymoron and an insult to our theology of grace and gift. I have no doubt we can and will do much better in the future.

The sexual polarities are the deepest archetypes of the soul. They determine what we pay attention to, what fascinates us, what wounds us, and what transforms us. The images of male and female are spiritual dynamite. God risks a lot in letting us be split and unsatisfied. We cannot seem to change these fascinations, no matter how hard we try or how loudly we moralize. God is clearly more comfortable with diversity than we are, and God's final goal and objective are much simpler. God and the entire cosmos are about two things: differentiation and communion. Physicists seem to know this better than theologians and clergy.

For twenty-five years I have been convinced that the renewal of the church and the reform of Christian morality are intrinsically tied to the rediscovery of Scripture and the unvarnished Jesus that we find there. In the end, we have no other foundation by which to hold people accountable. There is no perfectly "logical" position available. Without, at least, the seminal teaching in Jesus' life and ministry, all church authorities can do is shout louder and louder to make up for our lack of real authority and influence. As Richard Lacayo says, "To have influence is to gain assent, not just obedience; to attract a following, not just an entourage; to have imitators, not just subordinates." Jesus is willing to wait for the truth that demands assent and creates real followers and challenges to imitation. The church, clergy and laity, are much less patient because our goals are different.

The arguments of the anti-gay folks are often very well intentioned, but their goals and objectives seem to be different from those of Jesus. The arguments have to do with very secular concerns: control over chaos, majority rule, fear of the other, fear of the unknown, and idealization of a family unit that Jesus himself neither lived nor idealized. But then I remember that we are dealing with "the deepest archetypes of the soul," those electric sexual images that motivate us at the most intimate levels of our being. Such "totems and taboos" have a deep hold on every culture and every individual. We cannot expect Jesus' simplicity of intention to convert us so quickly, especially when he has had minimal success in the areas of greed, violence, use of power, and love of enemies *where he is absolutely forthright and hardly able to be misinterpreted.* Let's admit it, we have shown after two thousand years an amazing capacity for missing Jesus' central teaching. As he himself put it in the Gospel, "You strain out gnats and swallow camels" (Matt. 23:24). I would be afraid to say that, lest you think of me as bitter or negative, but fortunately I am only quoting *him.*

As a general rule, I would say that institutional religion tends to think of people as very simple, and therefore the law must be very complex to protect them in every situation. Jesus is exactly and consistently the opposite: He treats people as very complex—different in religion, lifestyle, virtue, temperament, and success—and keeps the law very simple in order to bring them to God.

A legal expert put him to the test: "Teacher, which commandment in the Law is the greatest?" He replied to him, "'You are to love the Lord your God with all your heart and all your soul and all your mind.' This is the first and foremost, and the second is like it: 'You are to love your neighbor as yourself.' On these two commandments hangs everything in the Law and in the Prophets."

(Matt. 22:35-40)

Again, I am glad that *he* said it! He really is our "Savior"! He saves us from our discomfort with common sense—and in this case he saves me from your judgments. If I would say this, apart from his authority, you would rightly accuse me of being simplistic, naive, and reductionistic. After all, religion is for the sake of social control, isn't it? Maybe civil religion *is* for the sake of social control. That is surely the way religion has been seen in most of history, by both clerics and county clerks.

Fortunately or unfortunately, depending on our objectives, Jesus does not give us much grist for the social-control mill. He is asking a different set of questions—a set of questions that leaves us with little sense of control, which is exactly why we call it "faith." A set of questions that takes away our private agenda, which is perhaps why we call it "hope." And a set of questions that remind us that we have not yet begun to love. For Jesus it is all about union—union with *what is*. How cleverly our moral pretenses free us from struggling with what is right in front of us. How ingeniously our ego protects itself from compassion and understanding. And how convenient that the 90 percent of the population that is heterosexual decides that homosexuality happens to be where sexual evil resides. Fortunately Jesus is not about scapegoating. He is about conversion and transformation, which is always about *me*. It is the Gospel that has led us to this dangerous freedom. It is Jesus who gives us this courage. It is our contemplative practice that cleans the lens and provides the hearing aid.

If this were cheap liberalism, I would be merely arguing for personal rights, economic justice, or sexual freedom. If this were mere ideology, I would need to line up my credible arguments and proofs. I have very few. I, like many of you, am only a disciple of the poor man from Nazareth. He has made me content with mystery. He has made me less afraid of chaos. He has told me that control is not my task. He, like the cosmos itself, is about two things: *diversity and communion*. The whole creation cannot be lying.

11

Being Christian about Homosexuality

John B. Cobb Jr.

↙

John B. Cobb Jr. is a son of the American South but was born in southern Japan. He earned M.A. and Ph.D. degrees from the University of Chicago Divinity School, where he studied process philosophy with Charles Hartshorne. From Chicago he went to the Hiawasee Circuit in north Georgia, where the largest of his seven congregations was known as Hog Creek. He also taught at Young Harris College before moving to Emory University for five years and then to Claremont School of Theology, from which he retired in 1990. He is widely regarded as the leading process theologian in the world and is greatly admired by students and colleagues alike. He is as famous for his incisive logic as for his gentleness and humility. He has written more than thirty-five books, among them *The Earthist Challenge to Economism: A Theological Critique of the World Bank* (1999), *Grace and Responsibility: A Wesleyan Theology for Today* (1995), and *For the Common Good: Redirecting the Economy toward Community, the Environment, and a Sustainable Future* with Herman E. Daly (1994).

↙

I have never been condemnatory of gay people. But for much of my career, I thought this negative virtue was sufficient. There were, I supposed, more important issues to deal with, so that this one could be largely ignored.

In the mid-seventies I was aroused from this complacency by a Mexican-American friend, Ignacio Castuera. Castuera had introduced me to Latin American liberation theology, and I admired his leadership in that field. But I was startled when he began speaking publicly against the moral condemnation of homosexual acts. Would it not be better, I asked him, to concentrate on the important issues raised by liberation theology? Would not his leadership there be compromised by involving himself in this very different and difficult question of sexuality?

Castuera replied that if he were to be true to liberation theology he must be especially concerned for those who are *most* oppressed in our society. He had come to the conclusion that these are gay people. He could not continue in silence about this for the sake of other oppressed people.

I had not thought in this way before. I was not completely ignorant of the suffering of gay people in our society. But until Castuera spoke, it had not occurred to me to think of them as the most oppressed people among us. Since then I have not been able to be silent or, at least, to be complacent in my lapses into silence.

Some may question whether gays and lesbians are the most oppressed group in our society. There is serious competition for that spot. But it is clear that whereas in most other oppressions the church has given at least some support to the oppressed, in this case the church has been the leader in the oppression. As a Christian this gives me special reason to share in repentance.

Most Christians now repent of much that we have done to make the lives of gay people miserable. There are many horrible features of our collective history, but none are worse than this. We are now ready to support the full civil rights of gays and lesbians and to do what we can to reduce the brutal acts that continue to endanger them. This agreement is a great gain that we should all be celebrating together. We find it hard to celebrate, however, because beyond this agreement we are caught in a painful disagreement as to whether all physical expressions of same-sex love, even if legally permitted, should be morally condemned.

Walter Wink makes clear that this moral condemnation is not grounded primarily on Scripture. There is equal or greater scriptural authority for many doctrines that the opponents of homosexual acts reject. The real ground for moral condemnation today, as in much of the Christian past, is the sense that they are unnatural and hence against

God's intentions. The strength of this sense comes from the revulsion felt by many heterosexuals at the thought of physical intimacy with members of their own gender. This personal revulsion causes revulsion also at the thought of others engaged in such activity.

Instead of wanting to reduce this revulsion, those who feel it typically desire that it remain strong and be widely shared. They fear that if it declines, some who are now inhibited by it, even their own children, might experiment with same-sex relations. Hence there is a strong desire to maintain the moral prohibition and to prevent those who violate it from functioning as role models for youth.

Those of us who are on the other side need to recognize the power of this involuntary revulsion in many just as we recognize the power of involuntary same-sex attraction in others. In seeking to avoid condemnation of the latter we should not condemn the former. But we cannot remain neutral with regard to what is to be done.

Whereas some consider it moral to act on their involuntary revulsion by condemning what revolts them, we believe that such condemnation is wrong. No one is to be blamed for feeling revulsion, but the decision to act on that revulsion in a way that injures others falls under moral criticism. The question is whether, in fact, homosexual acts are inherently immoral. We do not see any reason to suppose that this is so.

Instead of putting matters in purely moral terms, the Christian church should ask a different question. What does it recommend as a lifestyle to those whose sexual attractions are for members of their own sex? How is such a question to be answered?

The church should have in mind the total well-being of the person in question. It should also have in mind the well-being of actual or possible sexual partners. And it should be concerned for the larger social effects as well.

Consider the options. The church can recommend that natural feelings be denied and that the gay or lesbian person find a partner of the other gender. Presumably the church would encourage complete honesty, so that the partner would understand the limitations of the relations that can be expected.

In much of human history, marriage has been understood as a social relation having more to do with property and procreation than with the personal or sexual fulfillment of the partners. In that context this advice to gay and lesbian persons made sense. The question then arose as to whether it was permissible to seek in other ways the sexual satisfactions lacking in marriage or whether these hungers must be permanently repressed.

Although this arrangement is not impossible today, most Christians draw back from recommending it. Our understanding of the purposes of marriage is violated by it. And although there may be instances in which heterosexual marriage remains the best solution for one who is homosexually oriented, few of us would recommend it as the normative pattern for all.

This leads to the second option. The church can urge gay and lesbian persons to abstain from sexual activity throughout their lives. It would be foolish to suppose that large numbers would fully follow this teaching. But the church can create a climate that generates considerable feelings of guilt when this ideal is violated. Such guilt feeling does not always reduce sexual activity, but in some people it does.

If the church's goal is to reduce homosexual activity as much as possible, then this *may* be the correct teaching. But heterosexual Christians must ask why they demand so much suffering from those with a different sexual orientation. If they believe that sexual activity is something inherently bad, so that it is justified only in its connection with procreation, they will have reason to continue this teaching. But this is now a rare view. Most of those who urge abstinence on gays and lesbians regard sexual fulfillment as inherently positive in the case of heterosexuals. It is only their view that same-sex love is against nature that leads to its condemnation.

The practical consequence of both of the teachings noted is to encourage homosexual promiscuity. Church members can engage in many short-term liaisons without raising questions about their standing in the church. We tend not to pry into one another's private lives. But if a man brings another man to church with him regularly, if they give the same address and show signs of mutual affection, then there is likely to be a scandal. The dominant effect of church teaching is to encourage secret, temporary liaisons without commitment and to discourage long-term fidelity.

The third recommendation that the church can offer is that gay and lesbian persons look forward to finding partners of the same gender with whom to share their lives through thick and thin. In short, the same ideal that the church holds for heterosexual persons can apply to them. The implication is that the church should celebrate and support committed same-sex unions in the same way as heterosexual ones.

Needless to say, this would not solve all our problems with respect to sexual morality for our day. There is plenty of confusion about heterosexual marriages that don't work well. There are even serious arguments for separating sexual enjoyment from personal commitment. The institution of marriage may itself be evolving into something quite new.

But confusion about heterosexual mores today should not cause us to place a particular stigma on homosexuality. Our goal is human flourishing, holistic personal fulfillment for all. If, as most of us believe, this occurs best in the context of committed relationships that include sexual love, then we should teach this ideal without apology and without excluding a whole class of persons from it. Heterosexual and homosexual Christians can then work together to bring some healthy order out of the sexual chaos of our time.

Part Five

∽

Prophetic Voices

12

In God's House There Are Many Closets

Peggy Campolo

↔

Peggy Campolo is a writer and editor. She is a graduate of Eastern College and taught first grade prior to spending a number of years as a full-time wife and mother. She has also worked in real estate and public relations. She is a member of Evangelicals Concerned and serves on the Council of the Association of Welcoming and Affirming Baptists. Mrs. Campolo is a member of Central Baptist Church in Wayne, Pennsylvania, and on the Board of Directors of the Philadelphia Baptist Association. She is committed to working for justice for lesbian and gay people, especially within the church, and has spoken at colleges, conferences, and churches throughout the United States. Mrs. Campolo and her husband live in St. Davids, Pennsylvania. They are the parents of a son and a daughter and have four grandchildren.

↔

Gay people are not the only people who live in closets. People live in closets because they are afraid that they will not be loved or accepted if they are honest about who they are. My own time in a closet began when I was nine years old, and it lasted for thirty-eight years.

It was this way: I was raised in a Christian home—an American Baptist home in Philadelphia—and my beloved father was the pastor of my church. I grew up with people who said they prayed to God and heard from God. Most of them seemed to me to try to live their lives as they thought God wanted them to. My big problem was that even when I tried to get in touch, God just did not exist for me. It wasn't that God was calling me and I was saying no, even though I've heard many preachers say that's the way it always is. I wanted to be accepted by the people I knew in the church, and so I used to try very hard to be like them. Only God wasn't in it for me. Not then.

It was the custom in our church for the pastor to talk to the nine-year-old Sunday school class about making a public profession of faith, being baptized, and joining the church. In theory, any child was free not to do that, but the reality was that if I were honest, I alone would have been rejecting God, and, it seemed to me, my Dad, too.

It didn't take me long to decide what to do. I loved my Dad, and I didn't even know God. Daddy would be happy if I declared myself a Christian; God, if God did exist, might be upset about my pretending, but I decided to do what would please not only my father but everyone else I cared about. And I told myself that perhaps everyone just pretended they knew God because the idea of God was such a good one and was supposed to make people nicer. And so I pretended that Christianity was real to me, and I acted a part. I developed a great talent for evading direct questions and for giving answers that created a false impression, even as I carefully chose truthful words.

My husband got in trouble some years ago for saying that Jesus was a presence inside of every person whether that person was a Christian or not. Furthermore, Tony said that one place to find Jesus was in loving service to other people. Some in the Christian community argued that Jesus dwelt only in those who believed in him. There was actually a "heresy trial," held in Chicago, which ended with the "jury" saying that Tony was not a heretic but did need to be more careful about how he stated things. However, later that same year, I learned firsthand that Tony was right about where to find Jesus.

Helen Rue was a dear friend of mine. She was eighty-two years old and lived alone, except for her cat. She was a bright woman with a marvelous sense of humor, and she told wonderful stories of her travels and of the long ago days of her youth. Helen's world had grown smaller as she had gotten older, and I was the only person in it able to go to visit her regularly.

Then one night twelve years ago, Helen had a stroke and was rushed to the hospital. She did her best to keep up a brave front when I visited her, but as Helen grew more critically ill, she grew more afraid. She talked constantly about her fears for the future of her cat because she was unable to put her own terrors into words. Helen had always said she believed in God, but now she did not seem to have any assurance of heaven or peace about dying.

I spent many hours holding Helen's hand and listening. As the end drew near, I felt more inadequate than I ever have in my life. Helen needed God to die, and I needed God to help me if I was to be any comfort at all to my friend. I decided I would tell Helen all that I had ever heard about Jesus Christ and going to heaven. After all my years in church, I knew the story well. Helen held my hand for dear life, and I know she heard me. And, as I shared the story of God's grace and love with my dying friend, the presence of God became real to me—comforting, close, and very, very real.

I believe God did take Helen home to heaven, even as I know Jesus has remained with me. It was in my caring for Helen that God had found me. My husband's questioned theology about finding God in those who are in need or being oppressed became a reality to me that day in the hospital. God came into my life as I sought God for Helen. Jesus is waiting to be found in those who are in need— whether of food, of love, of respect, or of justice. None of us can be a loving presence to all of God's children. None of us can even perceive, let alone try to make right every wrong. But God has chosen for each of us those particular people God wants to love through us.

I have been heterosexual all my life. I don't have a gay son or a lesbian daughter. But after I became a Christian, God let me know that I was to love and speak out for my gay brothers and lesbian sisters in Jesus' name. And to my utter amazement, it dawned on me that God had been preparing my heart to do this long before I knew God.

Forty years ago I was a student at Abraham Lincoln High School in Philadelphia, and Tom was my friend. His hall locker was near mine, so we always met at the start and again at the end of the school day. Tom was a "comfortable" friend—I didn't worry about what I wore, how I looked, or the way what I said might come out when we talked. He liked me, and I can still remember how good it was to know that, at a time when I was not always sure I liked myself. He was a listening ear, a sympathetic heart, and in many ways a kindred spirit.

I didn't like it the day that some of the boys walking past our lockers upset Tom. All they did was to call his name as they sauntered past. But there was evil in their voices. "Tom-my, Tom-my," they called out, silly grins on their faces, eyes darting around to see who was watching their game. I followed Tom's example and tried to pretend that it hadn't happened. But I felt afraid and sad, and I knew that he did too. Variations of that ugly scene were played out more times than I care to remember. The horror to me was that I knew Tom was being harassed, not because of anything he had done, but because of who he was.

And then there were the jokes and innuendos, and people told me that Tom was "queer." If the answers I got to the questions I asked my folks at home were not really enough, it was made clear to me that the right thing to do was to go on being Tom's friend, and that his tormentors were wicked and wrong. But I already knew that. I also knew that I should take a stand for Tom. Sadly, in those days I did not take stands on much of anything. I was too afraid of being an outcast myself. I told people that Tom was a really nice person, and I begged my friends not to join in the teasing, but I didn't have what it took to turn my sadness into righteous indignation on Tom's behalf. And it was not until Jesus became real to me that I found out that it was God I needed to give me courage.

Twenty years ago, my husband and I went to Provincetown, Massachusetts, to see the whales. We had been "warned" that the charming village on the tip of Cape Cod was a mecca for gays and lesbians. I expected to ignore that, enjoy the whales, and go home. But I fell in love with Provincetown, and as I did, I realized that it was not in spite of the gay and lesbian culture there, but partly because of it. I have gone back every summer for twenty years.

You can fly to P-town from Boston on wonderful little Cessna airplanes that take you back to a pre-jet-plane era. The planes are small, and they fly so low that you can watch the ocean all the way. But it is the people I watch on our flights to P-town. Usually most of them are gay men, though there are some lesbians and a few straight folks like us. At the airport in Boston, I am always aware that not many of our fellow passengers appear to be as happy as Tony and I feel. Some seem to me to be carrying heavy burdens. Once the plane is on its way, a number of the passengers visibly brighten. At times, I imagine I hear a collective sigh of relief as we bid the straight and narrow good-bye, if only for a time.

Tony and I certainly share the joy of "getting away from it all," but *we* cannot even begin to comprehend what "it all" means to some of our fellow travelers. We like Provincetown because hardly anyone ever stops us to say, "Aren't you Tony Campolo?" I think about that, and I wonder if many of the other folks here are not happy for a similar reason.

Provincetown makes me think about the original meaning of the word *gay*. There is much to be joyful about there; it is one of the places where I feel happiest. Yet, knowing that most of the people in Provincetown, especially the couples, would not be so well treated in many places where I come from, I sometimes feel a sense of shame as folks smile at us, visit with us, and seem glad we have come. As a straight couple, we are most definitely in the minority, but no one seems to care. On our first visit to Provincetown, I remember saying to Tony, "What I feel here is something of what I have always imagined the church should be like, but isn't."

To be real about it, we who walk the streets of P-town do not even know each other. We certainly do not all love each other. But what I feel there makes me very aware of the aching void there is in most places on this earth, where people do *not* accept each other, nor are they kind. If acceptance can feel so holy, is not the lack of it an unholy thing?

I do not want to create the illusion that P-town really is any sort of heaven. It seemed so to me at first, and it must seem even more so to those vacationers who come there from their own private hells. But there is an underlying sadness there, too, and, sometimes, a touch of the ugly. Sometimes a caravan of pickup trucks roars through the main street, and ignorant individuals shout their anti-gay messages. For the most part, they are ignored. They pass through town and are gone. But they do leave a cloud—a reminder that much of the world is not as enlightened as Provincetown.

One afternoon, Tony met a man who recognized him as a preacher, and the two of them visited while I shopped. They talked theology and had a grand time. When I joined them, my husband tried to find out more about his knowledgeable new friend. The man did not give his name but simply said, "I was a priest in my former life. I used to love to talk about God. But when I told people who I really was, I couldn't be a priest anymore, and I don't usually think about God anymore, either. But it's been great to talk to you, friend." He was gone before more could be said, and some of his sadness remained with us.

We once spent an entire afternoon as the only customers at a small rooftop restaurant overlooking Cape Cod Bay. The young man behind the counter came out and joined us at our table. "Where's home for you?" Tony asked him. Too much time elapsed before the answer came: "Oh, my folks live in Iowa, but I can't go there anymore, so home is just wherever I happen to be, and I'm here now." "Why can't you go home?" Tony asked, really wanting to know. The look he got in response seemed to indicate that my husband must have spent most of his life on the moon.

There *is* sadness in Provincetown, amid the merrymaking and beauty. I see it in some of the faces I pass in the crowd. P-town is small enough that you keep on seeing the same people. The ads in the local papers and the handbills on the street tell me that this is a place where relationships are often over before they begin. I have the feeling that people are dancing too fast, relating too quickly, trying to "have it all" in two weeks, one night, or even an hour. I wonder where people go in the evenings to have what my mother used to call "a wholesome good time."

Having grown up as a Baptist minister's daughter, I think first of the churches. I've been to three of them there. Now one is an art gallery. The second is still a church, but most of the time the place is closed up and dark. Too bad, when you think of the hundreds of people who walk right past the door every summer evening, many of them looking for something to do and people to meet. We found the third church one Sunday morning when our children were still young enough to be vacationing with us. I remember several of the church people rushing over to find out if we were new in town. "You don't get many families, many 'regular' people in this town during the summer," one woman volunteered. As the conversation unfolded, it didn't take much to figure out who was not welcome in that place.

I think about the verse in the Bible that talks about fields being white and ready for harvest and the laborers being few. Provincetown is a place where I long to see an alive, welcoming Christian ministry start up—perhaps as a coffeehouse on the main street, a place where people could meet the real Jesus, who identifies with and loves oppressed people, not the one so often portrayed on television as a despiser of those who are different.

Provincetown made me a wiser person. As I got to know the place, I realized how narrow my straight life had been. I really did not know any openly gay people, and now I wanted to know some. It was rather like I had visited a foreign country, had a great time, and come home anxious to make friends with people of that nationality. And slowly that began to happen, as I let it be known that the status quo that existed for gay men and lesbians was unacceptable to me.

From time to time, a gay or lesbian student at Eastern College would find his or her way to my door. Most of them hurt badly. As I listened to their stories, a rage began to build in me. In all of my life, nothing had ever seemed so unfair as the lives these young men and women had to live. Nobody understood. Most of their parents were unfair, if indeed they had even found the courage to risk telling their parents. The college wanted them to be silent, and their churches just never seemed to be there for them. Either these young people had heard such condemnation from the pulpit that they knew better than to approach their pastors, or their pastors had been so silent on the issue that they had no idea what might happen if they took their heartaches to him or to her. So they hurt, in silence and often all alone. I marveled at how "together" many of them were able to be, in spite of the forces marshaled against them.

I wish I could tell you that my crusade for gay rights began back then, twenty years ago, but it did not. When my husband began to take a public stand on the issue, which seemed to me at the time to be liberal, I confess to having wished he did not feel the need to add yet one more controversial subject to his public life. I believed that gays and lesbians were entitled to the same rights and privileges I claimed for myself, including being able to marry, both legally and in the eyes of the church, whomever they chose as a life partner, but I still wasn't standing up to anybody or for anybody. It was not until I met Jesus that I found the courage to speak out for God's gay and lesbian children.

I have hope that someday soon there will be churches in places like Provincetown where the real Jesus is preached, where a biblical lifestyle is taught, and where loving relationships and the valuing of people are important; a place where lesbian and gay Christians can learn how God wants to bless their relationships and empower them to share their gifts with a world that needs them. I go to a church like that, so I know it's possible. And I have hope that some evening, when the little plane flies back to Boston from Provincetown, the smiles can remain on the faces and in the hearts of the gay and lesbian people going home, because they will be returning to a world that accepts them for who they are—children of God.

13

Liberty to the Captives and Good Tidings to the Afflicted

William Sloane Coffin

ﾉﾉ➚

William Sloane Coffin abandoned a career as a concert pianist to enter World War II. He followed with a stint with the CIA and a role in setting up the Peace Corps. For eighteen years he was chaplain of Yale University, then from 1977 to 1987 senior minister of the Riverside Church in New York City. Until his retirement he headed Sane/Freeze, now renamed Peace Action, the largest peace and human rights organization in the U.S. With Benjamin Spock he was indicted for his opposition to the Vietnam War. Over an illustrious career he has been in the forefront of virtually every struggle for justice and peace. His books include *A Passion for the Possible* (1993), *Living the Truth in a World of Illusions* (1985), and *The Courage to Love* (1983). He continues to be an itinerant preacher and professor, including visiting professorships at Vanderbilt and Lawrence Universities and the Pacific School of Religion. He lives in Strafford, Vermont, where he is once again enjoying being a concert pianist.

ﾉﾉ➚

Isaiah and Jesus came "to proclaim liberty to the captives, recovery of sight to the blind" and "to bring good tidings to the afflicted" (Isa. 61:1-2; Luke 4:18-19).

Let's start by asking, "Who are these captives, and what is it these days that holds them in bondage?"

I think it fair to say that most, if not all of us, tend to hold certainty dearer than truth. We want to learn only what we already know; we want to become only what we already are. And some of us even go so far as to embrace "The Principle of the Dangerous Precedent" put forth by the British academic who said, "Nothing should ever be done for the first time."

The result is an intolerance for nonconforming ideas that runs like a dark streak through human history. In religious history this intolerance becomes particularly vicious when believers divide the world into the godly and the ungodly; for them, hating the ungodly is not a moral lapse but rather an obligation, part of the job description of being a true believer.

Think how, for example, fleeing British persecution, our Puritan forebears sailed to America, only to become equally intolerant of religious ideas other than their own, which they enforced as the official faith of the Massachusetts Bay Colony. First they banned that early church dissenter, Anne Hutchinson, who, as she exited the church where the trial was held, said words haunting to this day: "Better to be cast out of the church than to deny Christ." (Everything churchly is not Christlike!)

In 1660 these Puritans went further, hanging Mary Dyer, a Quaker, for insisting, in effect, "Truth is my authority, not some authority my truth."

Three hundred years later, in the 1960s, this same intolerance made many Christians consider Martin Luther King Jr. more an agitator than a reconciler. And to this day most church bodies refuse to ordain not only gays and lesbians but *all* women. You'd think that if Mary could carry our Lord and Savior in her body, a woman could carry his message on her lips! As for the argument, repeated frequently by the Pope, that there were no women among the original twelve disciples: there were also no Gentiles.

Why all this intolerance? Because while the unknown is the mind's greatest need, uncertainty is one of the heart's greatest fears. So fearful, in fact, is uncertainty that many insecure people engage in what psychiatrists call "premature closure." These are those who prefer certainty to truth, those in church who put the purity of dogma ahead of the integrity of love. And what a distortion of the gospel it is to have limited sympathies and unlimited certainties, when the very reverse, to have limited certainties but unlimited sympathies, is not only more tolerant but far more Christ-

ian. For "who has known the mind of God?" And didn't
Paul also insist that if we fail in love we fail in all other
things?

The opposite of love is not hatred but fear. "Perfect love
casts out fear." Nothing scares me like scared people, for
while love seeks the truth, fear seeks safety, the safety so frequently found in dogmatic certainty, in pitiless intolerance.

So I believe the captives most in need of release, those
today whose closet doors most need to be flung open, are
really less the victims than their oppressors—the captives
of conformity, the racists, the sexists, the homophobes, all
who live in dark ignorance because their fears have blown
out the lamp of reason. These groundless fears that fence us
in remind me of this passage in E. B. White's journal, which
he wrote while living in Maine:

> A friend of mine has an electric fence around a piece of his
> land, and he keeps two cows there. I asked him one day
> how he liked his fence and whether it cost much to operate.
> "Doesn't cost a damn thing," he replied. "As soon as the
> battery ran down I unhooked it and never put it back. That
> strand of fence wire is as dead as a piece of string, but the
> cows don't go within ten feet of it. They learned their lesson
> the first few days.
>
> Apparently this state of affairs is general throughout the
> United States. Thousands of cows are living in fear of a
> strand of wire that no longer has the power to confine them.
> Freedom is theirs for the asking. Rise up, cows! Take your
> liberty while despots snore. And rise up too, all people in
> bondage everywhere! The wire is dead, the trick is exhausted.
> Come on out!

Yes, come on out, fearful people; the pasture is greener
where love prevails, and discords end, and the joys of unity
are proved. Come on out, Christians, because "For freedom
Christ has set you free."

Here's what many a Christian has learned: It is absolutely
right to love and learn from the sixty-six books of the Bible
(seventy-two if you're Roman Catholic), but it is wrong to
fear their every word, for *not everything biblical is Christlike.*
"Now go and smite Amalek. . . . do not spare them, but kill

both man and woman, infant and suckling, ox and sheep, camel and ass . . . . Thus says the Lord." Besides, we Christians believe in the Word made flesh, not in the Word made words. And for God's sake, let's be done with the hypocrisy of claiming "I am a biblical literalist" when everyone is a *selective* literalist, especially those who swear by the anti-homosexual laws in the Book of Leviticus and then feast on barbecued ribs and delight in Monday-night football, for it is *toevah*, an abomination, not only to eat pork but merely to touch the skin of a dead pig.

The Bible is the foundational document for all churches the world around. But I am convinced that "the Lord hath yet more light and truth to break forth from his/her word." And I am equally sure that no word of God is God's last word.

Now let us ask, "What are the good tidings the Lord brings to the afflicted, and particularly to gays and lesbians?" Isn't it terrible that so many church people are inhospitable to gays and lesbians because they are more sensitive to the fears of their fellow church members than to the suffering victims of their bigotry? It's terrible that most churches are more allied with the structures of power than with the victims of power. But not only does the Lord bring good tidings to the afflicted; she also binds up the brokenhearted. And who these days isn't brokenhearted when scores of friends have died of AIDS, "the destruction that wastes at noonday," to borrow a poignantly apt phrase from the Psalms?

The church enjoins the dying, "Don't die alone, die with Christ"; and none are more Christlike than those holding the dying in their arms. Nothing so moved me in my years in New York City as the courage of those dying of AIDS and the tenderness of their lovers and friends.

But almost equally moving has been the determination of the gay community, despite the "band playing on," despite setbacks in many states, to continue fighting for long overdue justice. The fight is hard, for as every liberation movement has learned to its sorrow, those who benefit from injustice are less able to understand its true character

than those who suffer from it. The enemy hence is not ignorance but self-interest. That's why the complacent need to
be disturbed, embarrassed, inconvenienced. I'm thinking
of the so-called good people who are "good" but within the
limits of their inherited prejudices and traditions. Someone
has to play Hamlet to their Horatio: "There are more things
in heaven and earth, Horatio, than are dreamt of in your
philosophy." Someone has to recall to them Jeremiah: "Woe
to those who say 'Peace, peace' where there is no peace";
and Jesus, too—"I came not to bring peace but a sword,"
the sword of truth, the only sword that heals the wounds it
inflicts.

But now comes the hard part, the part only gays and lesbians can play. The feminist movement in Norway has a
slogan, "Not to do to them what they did to us." In other
words, when people are screaming at you that you are a
moral pervert, can you so speak and act as to rob their position of any moral cogency? Surely this is one of the purposes
of "turn the other cheek." Experience has taught me that it
is the temper and spirit with which a movement conducts
itself rather than a particular action that makes the greatest
difference. Divested of moral pretensions, a prejudiced person becomes as Samson with his locks shorn.

Nonviolence does not mean turning yourself into a
doormat so that people can walk all over you. But it does
mean returning evil with good, violence with nonviolence,
hatred with a love that is obliged to increase upon pain of
diminishing.

Because all this he understood so profoundly, the great
agitator of the 1960s won the Nobel Peace Prize, and most
of America now celebrates a national holiday in his honor.
Because they, too, in Christlike fashion, returned evil with
good, both Anne Hutchinson and Mary Dyer have statues
in their honor in the center of the very city where the one
was banned and the other hanged, and Quakers are everywhere welcomed in churches.

The good tidings are that we live in a moral universe,
that God is not mocked, that human beings, after exhaust-

ing all the alternatives, finally do the right and wise thing. While many battles remain to be fought, if only because new fears arise when old fears have been dissipated, still African Americans have proved that the problem all along was one of white racism; women are proving that the problem all along was male chauvinism; and gays, lesbians, bisexuals, and transgendered people will one day succeed in proving that God's creation is far more pluralistic than prejudiced eyes have perceived.

So "blessing and honor, glory and power" be unto God and to our Lord Jesus Christ for proclaiming liberty to the captives of conformity and recovery of sight to the blindly prejudiced and for never failing to bring good tidings to the afflicted.

14

The Challenge of Nonconformity

Elise Boulding

~~

Elise Boulding is professor emerita of sociology of Dartmouth College and former secretary-general of the International Peace Research Association. Born in Oslo, Norway, she is the widow of Kenneth Boulding, mother of five children, grandmother of sixteen, and a member of the Society of Friends. She has worked internationally as a scholar and an activist on problems of peace and world order and is one of the outstanding sociologists of our time. She has been international chair of the Women's International League for Peace and Freedom and has served on the board of the United Nations University and the International Jury of the UNESCO Prize for Peace Education. A futurist, Dr. Boulding has conducted workshops on Imaging a World without Weapons. Among her titles are *The Future: Images and Processes* with Kenneth Boulding (1995), her monumental *The Underside of History: A View of Women through Time* (1992), and *Building a Global Civic Culture: Education for an Interdependent World* (1990).

~~

Reweaving webs of relationship is our main business in life. The process begins with the great separation that is birth. The ensuing bonding/reweaving between parents and newborn child is no simple process, because the individuality and conflicting needs of each assert themselves almost at once. All through life we go on bonding across differences, because we need others to make us whole. The tension involved in that bonding is part of the human condition, and we ignore or underestimate it at our peril. Loving isn't easy.

Those who are called to be nonconforming witnesses have a particularly complex task in reweaving relationships, because there are more differences to bond across. We know that many family webs were ruptured in wartime because families could not support sons who chose conscientious objection or nonregistration. A special witness of nonconformity is the gay/lesbian act of coming out. This involves publicly affirming the spiritual, social, and biological rightness of forming a primary bond with a person of one's own sex—women loving women and men loving men. It also means witnessing to the wholeness of each human being, man and woman. "There is neither Jew nor Greek, there is neither slave nor free, there is neither male nor female; for you all are one in Christ Jesus" (Gal. 3:28).

That witness to oneness is something all of us can share with lesbians and gays, at the same time acknowledging that primary bonding with a person of one's own sex is a special case of the sexual bonding of the species. Some heterosexuals unite so strongly with the gay witness for wholeness and against the gender distinctions that warp personhood that they declare themselves "spiritual gays." That fellowship of concern is important to gay people because their nonconformity results in the breaking of many family and community bonds as family and friends reject the nonconforming position. The rejection causes pain and anguish only heightened by a public unwillingness to acknowledge even the legitimacy of the pain, let alone the position taken.

It is important for Friends to understand the consequences for those in their midst who make the nonconforming choice of being publicly gay. Because recent decades have been a relatively easy time for Friends—a time of respectability—many have forgotten or never knew the pain of nonconformity. Yet many of us who were rearing children at the close of World War II spent much time thinking about how to rear them to be war-rejecting nonconformists. The post-Hiroshima world looked very bleak indeed. It was not something we wanted our children to be part of. We wanted them to help shape and be citizens of a very different world. In those years I read about the lives of many peace-committed social-change activists, hoping to find some clues to what gave them strength for nonconformity. I found certain common elements in the childhood of each: (1) an experience of solitude, separation from society in childhood, whether through illness, isolated living, family differentness, or for other reasons; (2) an experience of close attachment to some adult while young, inside or outside the family; and (3) a capacity to daydream, to envision a different and better world, which became the basis for reconnection with society-as-it-could-be. The combination of having experienced both separation and bonding seemed to make the vision of the other possible, and drew the nonconforming activist to the work of reweaving the social web on behalf of the vision. Many Quaker gays and lesbians fit that model of social change activists.

Today the Quaker gay community has a special calling to reweave the social web on behalf of gay people's vision. Their nonconforming witness comes out of the pain of their isolation, from the strength of the love they have known, and from the image of a different future social order. Many Friends are not only unaware of the social nature of the gay witness, they are unaware it is a witness at all. Gay Quakers' nonconforming position is all too often seen only in terms of human rights. In fact the gay position represents a deepening and enriching of Quaker testimonies on equality, nonviolence, community, and simplicity, and as such deserves our respect, love, and support.

Let us look at gay and lesbian people's contribution to the Quaker testimonies:

Equality: The gay position goes beyond generally affirming equality in human relations. It deals with the specifics of the subordination of women to men, and to the specifics of all subordination—women to women and men to men. It sees equality with x-ray eyes, in relation to age, class, ethnic, or cultural differences. Most of us affirm the testimony to equality without doing anything very complicated to maintain it. Gayness, however, sets aside all the conventional signs and symbols associated with traditional gender-based roles—which are also signs and symbols of inequality—and calls for crafting relationships that fully acknowledge the other as equal. Nothing can be taken for granted. It is only when one looks at society through the eyes of a gay person that one realizes how much unthinking social subordination goes on in daily life. Yes, much of it is not life-threatening, but it is all part of the web of inequality. Early Friends took objection to hat honor (they refused to take off their hats in the presence of their superiors, even the king) and the honorific "you" with the same seriousness that gay people take objection to gender and status honoring.

Community: On the one hand, the gay witness to community permits no gender barriers to assumption of responsibility. On the other hand, it gives a new positive definition to age-old customs in every society of women gathering with women and men gathering with men in various settings and for various occasions. The community of women helping women has been a positive nurturant force in society, and so has the community of men helping men (when the latter has not involved warmaking). At present we move bumpily between same-sex and heterosexual groupings in our social enterprises. Gay people can help enrich our understanding of the potentialities and strengths of each type of grouping.

Simplicity: What many gays and lesbians bring to the witness of simplicity is not only a rejection of accumulation for its own sake, but a highly developed aesthetic sense for the patterning of our environment. Whether the general public knows it or not, gay people have made tremendous contributions to our society in the arts and humanities, and the tradition of doing so goes back a long way. Quaker "plain" turns beautiful.

Celebration: Another contribution of gayness that infuriates many is the gay gift for celebration, for joyfulness, for the dance of life. A gay dance is a very different affair from most public dances, open and welcoming to all ages in the best tradition of Quaker family dancing—a needed counterweight to the Quaker tendency toward gloom. Behind the gay joyfulness, won at great cost, is the deep spiritual experience of accepting one's own identity, of being able to say aloud and in public, with pride and grace, "I am gay."

Discipline: Finally, there is the witness of the disciplined life. *Discipline* is a hard word to understand. By "disciplined life" I mean a careful intentionality, a choosing, a discerning, in all one's actions. Gays and lesbians who choose the responsibility of being publicly out about their sexual orientation set aside conventional social role assignments and thus subject themselves to a constant process of discernment. Life has to be organized and directed toward the living of the new wholeness, to the crafting of the new person.

Reweaving the web at the family level is where broken bonds are most painful. Gay and lesbian Quakers have parents, grandparents, brothers, sisters, cousins, aunts, and uncles like everyone else, but they are often (though not always) treated as black sheep. When they form couples and marry, they would often like to be married under the care of their local meeting but may find it difficult to communicate that wish. They sometimes have children from former marriages, sometimes adopt children, sometimes take in singles with children—and very often serve in the time-honored role of extra parenting adult. Many of them work with children as teachers and caregivers. Like the celibate Shakers of an earlier era, many gays and lesbians love children and take care that there are children in their lives.

What is a family? In the broadest sense it is a complex of households of relatives spread widely over one or more continents, some of which carry out the functions of reproduction. In theory these households keep in touch with and care about one another; from time to time they meet for family reunions. Sometimes gays and lesbians are invited to family reunions, sometimes not. Most households develop an additional "extended family" of friends who are "like one of the family." Such extended families are especially important to gay people. Sometimes Friends meetings organize extended family groups as part of the ministry of the meeting community, and gays and lesbians are often part of these.

The sad truth, however, is that gay people usually find themselves outside the family networks they most value, cut off from people they love, by the social obsession that gays and lesbians are "unnatural," pathological people. The strengths gay people have to offer their families are so many, and the rewards for their families of experiencing reconnection so great, one can only hope that increasingly families will reconsider mending ruptured relationships with gay offspring.

Many gays and lesbians have special gifts and insights regarding family relationships that can strengthen both their families of origin and meeting families. These parallel the testimonies mentioned earlier. First and foremost is the testimony to equality in couple relationships. Because they accept no gender-based status differentials, same-sex couples are challenged with crafting an equality of relationships that few heterosexual partnerships achieve. Needless to say, it is typically based on a continuing openness to each other. At the same time, however, it must be remembered that most gay couples live under stress. Same-sex couples long for stability and long-term relationships, but they occasionally experience the same painful marital dissolutions that heterosexual couples go through.

Same-sex couples are denied the buffering effect that extended families provide young couples when troubles arise. The longing to reweave the family web and feel the support of parents and extended biological family is one of the most poignant aspects of being gay. The longing to reweave the web is not only personal; it is social. Many gays and lesbians long to help shape a society in which human beings and families are more gentle with one another.

How can the family web be rewoven? Caring about one's family does not in itself bring about reconnection, or there would be few gays and lesbians separated from their families, so a kind of negotiation would seem in order. When differences are strong, mutual respect is the scarcest resource. In the case of gay people, parents often do not respect their gayness, and gays and lesbians themselves begin (sometimes unconsciously) to lose respect for their parents' continuing inability to accept their sons and daughters in new identities. For gay people to work on ways to let their families know they respect them may be an important part of the process of winning respect in return.

Negotiation requires discovering common interests. One strong common interest between gay people and their families is the hidden love on both sides that longs to find expression. It can be drawn out with patience. Negotiation also requires a willingness to "give" on matters of lesser concern. What can gay people "give" on? What can their families "give" on?

Learning new ways of approaching gender identity and new ways for men and women to live and work separately and together in building the peaceable kingdom is urgent for us all. The gays and lesbians among us can help us in our learning and in our doing. It is time for them to be freed from the stereotype of embattled victims fighting for the right to be who they are and instead to be accepted as co-workers in reweaving the social web for us all.

Part Six

⁓

Acceptance and Blessing

16

Baptism, Bread, and Bonds: Church Rites for Gay and Lesbian Christians

Ignacio Castuera

✌⌐

Ignacio Castuera is currently pastor of the North Glendale United Methodist Church in Glendale, California. He received his Ph.D. in religion from the Claremont School of Theology. Dr. Castuera served pastorates in Mexico, Hawaii, and California and has traveled extensively, lecturing and preaching in Latin America, Europe, Japan, and most of the states in the United States. In 1992 he edited *Dreams on Fire, Embers of Hope,* a book of sermons preached on the weekend following the Los Angeles riots. The book was one of the top ten on religion that year and has been used extensively in sociology classes in several universities.

✌⌐

I grew up in Puebla, Mexico, in the bosom of a devoted and committed Roman Catholic family. Very early in my life I began experiencing a kind of marginalization that eventually would lead me to understand all marginalizations.

We lived in a very poor neighborhood, but my parents' values were not the values of the majority of the people around whom we lived. My mother made our clothes by hand, using patterns she made by taking apart our clothes and then transferring the pattern to a newspaper. Then she would add a few inches around the whole pattern to account for our growth. We always wore new, clean clothes that set us apart from the rest of the children in the area. To boot, my parents favored shorts over trousers, so we were the only children with short pants in the streets of our neighborhood and in our schools.

When I first started school, my mother negotiated a scholarship in a Salesian elementary school. The majority of the children were upper middle class, and my background of poverty could not hide me in spite of my mother's efforts to make me appear as "one of them." I obtained the highest grades in my classes, including three consecutive catechism championships, but that, rather than earning me the respect of my peers, pushed me further to the margins.

In fourth grade my mother transferred us to the public school system. From the very beginning I felt unaccepted and distrusted because I had come from a private school and because I continued to get the highest marks in school. It was there that I discovered that there was someone who was disliked more than I was. He was called all kinds of names I had not heard in the parochial school I had attended, and all the kids laughed at him and showed him absolutely no respect. I befriended him and discovered that he was nice, intelligent, and caring. I also realized that all the names other students called him had to do with his sounding like a girl and acting in effeminate ways. I did not understand anything about sexuality, having been sheltered in the parochial school, but I understood about not belonging, and that created a common bond.

At the age of thirteen I went to a Halloween party at the Methodist Church in Puebla, having promised my mother that I would not go into the sanctuary, since we were not supposed to go near any Protestant church. I discovered that the people I had been taught to fear were in fact kind, "normal" people. The teenagers at the party were a lot like me, but their faith in Christ seemed more real and personal than my Roman Catholic experience. I announced to my parents that I was going to attend the Sunday school and the children's service on Sunday. After a long and difficult discussion, it was decided I would first go to Mass, and then I could visit the Methodist church. I loved it from the very beginning and decided to become a Methodist in a country that was 95 percent Roman Catholic. This introduced me to yet another way of being a marginal person.

Fortunately, through all these changes my grades were good. I learned English, interpreted for American missionaries, and in 1960 received an invitation to come to the United States to the Spanish American Institute, a Methodist educational organization in Gardena, California, eleven miles south of downtown Los Angeles. There I expected to finally find myself at the center rather than the margins, only to discover that I was now a "minority" because of my Hispanic background.

Looking back I believe that all these minority experiences prepared me to understand the marginalization of gay and lesbian people in our society. It was easy for me to identify with all who suffer simply because they are different. The message of Martin Luther King Jr. and César Chávez resonated with me immediately even though I had not grown up in this country. When the Stonewall Rebellion took place in 1969,* I was more than ready to support the efforts of gay and lesbian people to gain full acceptance in society.

Providentially I attended a seminary, Claremont School of Theology, that prepared me well to deal with all social ills and with the sin of homophobia. We visited Glide Memorial Church in San Francisco as part of a summer class I took in 1966 and met with people in the recently formed Council on Religion and the Homophile. One of our "guides" to the San Francisco gay scene was a former Presbyterian minister who showed us both the "gay" and the painful side of living as a homosexual even in Baghdad by the Bay.

I started full-time ministry in 1968 in Hawaii. The Vietnam War was raging, and I found myself in the midst of the war resistance community. Several of the most committed antiwar activists I met were gay and lesbian people who

---

*In June 1969 New York police raided the Stonewall Inn, a gay bar. Police raids on gay bars were common at the time, but that night the bar's patrons fought back, creating a riot that lasted three days. The Stonewall Rebellion received national media attention at the time, and today it is considered a touchstone for the gay, lesbian, bisexual, and transgender civil rights movement.

extrapolated from their pain and decided to counter all dehumanizing enterprises. One of my great heroes was Lyle Loder, a young gay man from Kansas, who wanted to become an ordained pastor but who refused to live his life in a closet. Lyle was a crusader against all forms of oppression and never hesitated to speak up and act whenever he perceived that a wrong was being committed. During the first grape boycott by César Chávez's Farm Workers Union, Lyle was present at a luncheon sponsored by a church-related organization. Noticing that the salad being served had grapes, Lyle proceeded to remind us all that as a conference and as a denomination we had decided to support the Farm Workers Union. Lyle then proceeded to pull out all the grapes from the salad and toss them into the garbage can. With examples like that one it was very easy for me to extrapolate from my history of alienation and empathize with gay and lesbian causes. I further realized that the budding liberation theology that had started in communities of color and among women could apply to gay and lesbian Christians.

In 1972 my denomination started down a path of internecine theological and cultural wars around the issue of ministry with gay and lesbian persons. The Board of Church and Society presented a draft for consideration and approval by the General Conference dealing with human sexuality. It contained a compassionate sentence about the sacred worth of homosexual persons: "Homosexual persons, no less than heterosexual persons, are individuals of sacred worth." A clever phrase was introduced from the floor by a delegate from one of the Southern conferences creating a distinction between homosexual persons and homosexuality as a condition: "though we do not condone homosexuality and consider it incompatible with Christian teaching."

Every four years since then, attempts have been made to remove the incompatibility clause, but all we have succeeded in doing is to add modifications that emphasize the ministry to all persons that Christians are called to carry out.

The paragraph in the 1996 Discipline reads:

Homosexual persons no less than heterosexual persons are individuals of sacred worth. All persons need the ministry and guidance of the church in their struggles for human fulfillment, as well as the spiritual and emotional care of a fellowship that enables reconciling relationships with God, with others, and with self. Although we do not condone the practice of homosexuality and consider this practice incompatible with Christian teaching, we affirm that God's grace is available to all. We commit ourselves to be in ministry for and with all persons.

In the 1980s I found myself in the midst of the AIDS pandemic trying to respond with the resources available to me as the district superintendent of the Los Angeles district. I wrote the first major article by a church official addressing the AIDS pandemic in the *Circuit Rider,* the United Methodist journal for pastors. In the article I suggested that we needed to treat this disease as a medical issue and that in the meantime we needed to provide all the necessary pastoral support that persons with AIDS needed.

In 1985, after five years as the district superintendent of the Los Angeles district of the United Methodist Church, I requested the bishop to appoint me to the First United Methodist Church of Hollywood. During my superintendency I had grown closer to Lyle Loder and to a dynamic group of committed gay and lesbian Christians. Hollywood United Methodist Church, as it is now known, became the home of the first meeting of Affirmation Los Angeles and in 1991 became the fiftieth Reconciling Congregation in United Methodism. Reconciling Congregations are committed to a complete ministry to gay, lesbian, and bisexual Christians and their families. In 1997 there were more than 110 Reconciling ministries in United Methodism. Parallel organizations in mainline denominations are also increasing the number of parishes where gay and lesbian Christians can worship without fear of being marginalized, ostracized, or otherwise persecuted.

In the midst of my ministry in Hollywood I was called upon to perform rituals of support for gays and lesbians. I baptized several gay men, distributed communion to all gay people who came to the communion rail, and presided over rituals of remembrance and resurrection for many who died as a consequence of HIV/AIDS. I also presided over several rituals of commitment to love and companionship sometimes referred to as "unions," other times as marriage ceremonies. I never imposed any restrictions on the kinds of rituals and ministries I performed for gays and lesbians or straight parishioners. To me this is consistent with the ministry of Christ and congruent with the disciplinary requirement to "be in ministry for and with all persons."

In 1990 I was summoned to my bishop's office to talk about the same-sex weddings that had been taking place in our church. Bishop Jack Tuell, one of United Methodism's premier designers and defenders of *The Book of Discipline* asked me about the gay weddings. I told him that indeed, there had been several same-sex unions/weddings, and that I had presided over a few of them. He suggested I cease and desist doing so in the church but granted that I could still perform some sort of private ceremony in other locations. My response to Bishop Tuell went along the following lines: "Bishop, in United Methodism we recognize only two sacraments, Baptism and Holy Communion. If I were to refuse to administer either of these sacraments to gay and lesbian persons, it would be your duty to bring charges against me for failure to carry out my ministry. If we so treat the sacraments, why should I, or any other pastor, be prevented from presiding over the exchange of the incredibly daring promises to stay in a loving relation, 'for better, for worse, for richer, for poorer, in sickness and in health, till death us do part'?" Bishop Tuell was silent for a while and then said with a smile, "Ignacio, you always have very good arguments." I did not take his response to mean agreement, so I offered him a compromise. I would only preside over ceremonies at the church whenever bona fide members of the congregation asked me to do so, otherwise I would follow my conscience about presiding over same-sex unions away from the church.

In October of 1995, more than a year after Bishop Tuell's retirement, I was asked by the staff of *The Cristina Show*, one of the most popular Spanish-language shows, to preside over the unions of a lesbian couple and a gay couple. The educator in me could not refuse the opportunity to address a viewership of more than 200 million people in the United States, Latin America, and Europe. I presided over two ceremonies that were not sensationalist and included serious dialogue and, I hope, some education. Hispanic pastors from my denomination have put pressure on my bishop, Roy Sano, and on the institutions where I teach to remove me from my responsibilities. Whenever dialogue has been possible, I have outlined for those who oppose my point of view the same argument I presented Bishop Tuell almost a decade ago.

In 1996 the General Conference, the highest legislative body in my denomination, outlawed same-sex unions. Fifteen bishops issued a statement of conscience decrying the fact that there was a gap between the legislative position that they as bishops have to uphold and the dictates of their compassionate consciences. In January 1997 I and fourteen other United Methodist ministers issued a similar statement calling for support for those whose ministry requires that they be present and available for the liturgical needs of gay and lesbian persons in their parishes. I now pastor a church where the probability of a gay or lesbian couple asking me to marry them is infinitesimal, but there are many of my colleagues for whom participation in rituals of Baptism, Bread, and Bonds will be required of them by the gay and lesbian members of their parishes. I would hope that as they deal with the sacraments, they equally extend their support for rituals of love and commitment.

17

Same-Gender Covenants

M. Mahan Siler Jr.

∽

M. Mahan Siler Jr. is originally from Tennessee and is an American Baptist minister. After a variety of pastorates, he served for ten years as a staff member and then director of the School for Pastoral Care at North Carolina Baptist Hospital in Winston-Salem. Since 1983 he has been pastor of the Pullen Memorial Baptist Church in Raleigh, North Carolina. He has been a visiting professor at Southern Baptist Theological Seminary, Southeastern Baptist Seminary, and the Divinity School at Duke University. With his wife, Janice, a marriage and family counselor, he has four children. In late February 1993, Pullen's congregation voted to conduct a worship ceremony to bless the commitment between a gay church member and his partner. The controversy over Pullen Church's decision led to its expulsion from the Southern Baptist Convention and the loss of about a tenth of its members. The event was described in detail in *Enlarging the Circle: Pullen's Holy Union Process*, by Patricia V. Long, and *Celebration of Same-Gender Covenants*.

∽

I would never have predicted that our congregation would vote to bless a gay relationship in the name of God. Sharing the sequence of experiences that led me to propose such a controversial ritual to my congregation is personally clarifying. Perhaps the results, as well, will be useful to others who are grappling with the church's ministry to gay Christians in our day.

For ten years I was on the staff of the School of Pastoral Care at North Carolina Baptist Hospital in Winston-Salem. As a pastor counselor, I was, on occasion, invited into the particular pain that gays and lesbians face in our society. Most of them had internalized the prejudice of society in the form of self-hatred and fear. My first step began in those years.

During a public hearing on discrimination against gays and lesbians sponsored by the Human Relations Commission of Raleigh in 1986, I took another step. Being placed on the docket at the conclusion of the evening, I sat through two hours of testimony. Again and again I heard persons, mostly gays and lesbians, go public with their experiences of discrimination. Particularly alarming were the illustrations of frequent condemnation from the pulpit coupled with rejection from congregations. For these gay persons the church had been a sign of hostility, not a source of reconciling love.

After hearing that evening so many back-to-back examples of church abuse, a personal decision began to take shape within me. It was a second step taken: to come out of my own kind of closet and give public voice to what I had come to believe privately. The most compelling and propelling influence was from gay Christians who desired to affirm both identities—being Christian, being gay.

It began with an unsigned letter from a member who anticipated some reference to homosexuality in a series of sermons I was offering on human sexuality.

Dear Pastor,

Some of us, whom the church has driven into exile, are waiting to hear whether we are really the children of God or merely the skeletons in the family closet. Are we, too, made in the divine image, or are we some grotesque cosmic error? The crucial issue is not what we do or refrain from doing. That is a different matter. The issue is what we are, and whether our acceptance as participants in the community of faith is, as it often seems, contingent upon our letting others know who we are. We have no record of Jesus having spoken directly to our situation. The Old Testament and the Southern Baptist Convention are unequivocal. Is "abomination" the final word?

—A familiar stranger

This "familiar stranger" soon afterward identified herself as Pat and became a trusted partner in this third step of learn-

ing from the stories of new gay Christian friends. I heard
Pat's dilemma in so many of them: "Do I tell or not tell? . . .
and tell whom? . . . and at what cost? If I come out of the closet, will I have to come out of the church as well? Will I lose
my job? Or if not, will I lose my friendships in the job? Could
I ever hold a public, even controversial, job without wondering if my sexual orientation would be discovered and used
against me? And my family: how honest can I be at home?"

But at the core of Pat's dilemma was her theological
query: "Is my sexuality as a gay person also a gift from
God, a grace to be received with gratitude and expressed in
responsible commitments? Am I also a child of God, bear-
ing the image and capacity of God to love and be loved? Or
am I some grotesque cosmic error?"

The next step was more intellectual. Is a person's basic
sexual orientation primarily given, thereby discovered, or
is it chosen? Specifically, does an individual choose to be
gay or discover himself or herself to be gay? My answer,
based on what I heard and read, was yet another step to
take: for most people, it seems, one's basic sexual orientation is a given and cannot be changed at will. Behavior can
be changed, controlled, and managed; one's essential sexual
preference cannot.

If that is true, I concluded, then how cruel of the church
to judge as an "abomination" what is given in the physical
and emotional development of a person. How uncharacter-
istic of God to allow a few to be inherently gay, yet condemn
any acknowledgment and responsible, caring expression of
that gift. This became another step.

But how about the Bible? Interpreting the Scripture
regarding homosexuality was a step more complex than I
can adequately address in this article. I've come to believe
that the biblical mandate is to love the gay person—to con-
front behavior when it is destructive, to support behavior
when it is caring, to offer the alienated, both straight and
gay, our reflection of God's love.

The blessing by the church of a same-sex union became
for me a final logical step. I saw the ritual as a positive

affirmation of a lifelong covenant. It enables the same affirming support from family and faith community available to those of us who form heterosexual marriage covenants. And support is so minimal in our society. Little encouragement is offered to gay people who desire monogamous, loving relationships. Few models of committed relationships exist for gays and lesbians. The church easily joins the chorus of those lamenting the promiscuity associated with "one-night stands." Or, more often, we have stood by in silence while gays are slammed with the label "gay lifestyle"—meaning, of course, promiscuity. Why, I wondered, is the church so culture-bound when we have such a rich tradition of covenant-making to offer?

The blessing of same-sex covenants, it seemed to me, was a place for our congregation to stand. We live by our covenants—with God in Christ and with each other. The nurture of faithful covenants, the healing of broken covenants, and the healing of those broken by broken covenants I understand to be our reason for being. Of all institutions, I concluded, churches should encourage the blessing and nurture of such covenants.

This I came to believe. I have come to appreciate this additional ritual, with all the ministry only rituals can release. In the practice of this ritual, I have discovered gay and lesbian Christians who were yearning to come to themselves, to church, and to God.

But I mark this surprise. All along I thought that gays and lesbians were the victims in need of our care. We were the givers; they were the receivers. Well, yes . . . but not so much as we, our congregation, were in need of their gifts of gratitude and grace. My surprise must have been the surprise of the lawyer upon hearing Jesus' story about the "good Samaritan." The "despised one" was the one who cared most. The condemned one did the saving. My experience, indeed our experience as a congregation, had this Jesus twist to it.

We hadn't counted on the "closet" door opening in our direction.

Afterword

ᴌᴅ

In the final analysis, Jesus is the model for Christians. Jesus' silence on homosexuality is not so significant; he was silent on many things. But he was not silent regarding compassion toward those who had been marginalized and rejected as a class, or group, or occupation. If we attempt to enter the mind of Jesus, we can scarcely conclude otherwise than that he would have sided with the humanity and dignity of those whose sexual orientation was same-sexed.

Wherever we come out on this issue, however, that same spirit of Jesus surely calls us to respect, honor, and be civil toward those with whom we differ. No moral matter should be regarded as so urgent as to permit dehumanizing and demonizing our opponents. Jesus did not speak out on homosexuality, but he did command us, openly and unequivocally, to love our enemies—even when they choose to behave unlovingly toward us. As John Cobb urges in his essay, we can act Christianly toward one another while still holding to our convictions.

There is no room for lovelessness, hatred, or intolerance. God is confronting both sides of this controversy with an opportunity to transcend our verbal violence and put-downs, and to learn how to love, cherish, and value those whose positions are different from our own. We can treat this controversy, not as a sign of the church's decadence or its disobedience, but as a marvelous opportunity to learn to love as Jesus commanded us to love.